THE LOST BOOK OF KING ARTHUR

SIMON KEEGAN

NEW HAVEN PUBLISHING LTD UK

The Lost Book of King Arthur

First Edition
Published 2016
NEW HAVEN PUBLISHING LTD
www.newhavenpublishingltd.com
newhavenpublishing@gmail.com

Back cover photo © Dominic Coyne, Young Graduates for Museums and Galleries programme August 2007 (Wikimedia Commons)

Cover design © Pete Cunliffe
pcunliffe@blueyonder.co.uk

newhaven
publishing

With thanks to

My mum and dad for encouraging my Arthurian quest and letting nearly every childhood holiday be to places of Arthurian interest. From Tintagel in Cornwall, to St Gildas in Brittany to Ruthin in Wales, you helped my adventures be magical.

To my wife Sally for patiently indulging me on yet another hair-brained plan and dragging our kids round Hadrian's Wall and Roman York while Daddy takes pictures of rocks.

To my publisher Teddie Dahlin for giving me a chance and graphic designer Pete Cunliffe for carrying out my front cover design briefs perfectly.

To Elizabeth Gracen for making me realise that some legends are true. The once and future immortal.

To everyone who supported my first book Pennine Dragon. You know who you are.

Whilst occupied on many and various studies, I happened to light upon the History of the Kings of Britain, and wondered that in the account which Gildas and Bede, their elegant treatises, had given of them, I found nothing said of those kings who lived here before the Incarnation of Christ, nor of Arthur, and many others who succeeded after the Incarnation; though their actions both deserved immortal fame, and were also celebrated by many people in a pleasant manner and by heart, as if they had been written. Whilst I was intent upon these and such like thoughts, Walter, archdeacon of Oxford, a man of great eloquence, and learned in foreign histories, offered me a very ancient book in the British tongue, which, in a continued regular story and elegant style, related the actions of them...

Geoffrey of Monmouth, 1136AD

CONTENTS

PART ONE

WHO WAS ARTHUR?

INTRODUCTION

In 2016, on the 1500th anniversary of the Battle of Badon, I published Pennine Dragon: The Real King Arthur of the North.

It was the first book in those 1500 years dedicated purely to the hypothesis that Arthwys ap Mar (Arthur Penuchel) was the historic King Arthur.

In the short time since the book was published, a few things have moved on. The site of 'Camulod' at Slack (Outlane golf course) has now received extra protection, thanks to local archaeologists.

I have also visited a number of the battle sites and narrowed down some of my searches, including the precise location for the battles of Badon, Dubglas and Glein.

Now that the reader understands that the exploits of King Arthur are ultimately traceable to Arthwys ap Mar, we can start to see how the puzzle formed.

Over the years there have been many lost sources relating to Arthur – Geoffrey of Monmouth for example mentioned "a very ancient book" that he translated in writing his History of the Kings of Britain. And Nennius too talked of lost sources that he used in presenting his work on Arthur. We also know that works like the Annales Cambrae must have been derived from earlier sources. But what were they?

By understanding that Arthur Pendragon is to be identified with Arthur Penuchel, or Arthwys ap Mar as he is known in the king lists, we can finally understand what these books contained.

King Arthur for beginners

King Arthur is perhaps the greatest legendary hero in European history and he is made all the more intriguing by the efforts to discover whether he was real - and if so, who he was.

Arthur's reign would sit within the so-called Dark Ages, between the Romans leaving Britain in around 400AD and the full Saxon conquest by around 600AD. No coins were minted in this time, there is no coin marked "Artorius Rex" despire this book's cover!

Much of what we think of as being the Arthurian legend comes from Le Morte D'Arthur (the death of Arthur) by Sir Thomas Mallory in the 15th century. Characters like King Arthur, Queen Guinevere, Sir Lancelot, Merlin, Morgan, Tristram, Bedevere and Mark are found in their typical form in this book.

Mallory essentially condensed two sets of Arthurian romances. He took the British work of Geoffrey of Monmouth (Arthur, Uther, Guinevere) and combined them with French works by the likes of Chretien de Troyes, who wrote in the 12th century.

Geoffrey and Chretien did not invent their characters from scratch. While both added to the narrative, the core themes were already there. Geoffrey took much of his work from earlier historical works like Nennius' Historia Brittonum, written in around 800AD, the Annales Cambrae, from around 900AD and the work of Gildas from around 550AD (I am rounding off dates for simplicity).

Nennius is often regarded as the first 'historical' mention of Arthur. He calls him the Dux Bellorum (battle duke) and lists 12 battles Arthur won against the Saxons. The Annales Cambrae also list two battles and date Arthur.

From the available sources we can imagine a flourit of around 500AD for Arthur, right in the middle of the Dark Ages.

However it is not fair to suggest Arthur was not recorded until hundreds of years after his death. His first historic mention is by Anierin in around 580 – well within living memory of the man. There are also early Welsh sources like the tale of Cullhwch, Pa Gur and the Book of Taliesin that suggests Arthur was well established in the centuries after his death.

Knights like Lancelot, Kay, Bedevere and Gawain have their equivalents in earlier British heroes like Llwch Llaeminauc, Cei, Bedwyr and Gwalchmai.

Over the years there have been various theories as to who Arthur was, from the sublime to the ridiculous. He has been identified with around 20 different historic kings, generals and princes, as well as with gods and comets, and accused of being total fiction.

In Pennine Dragon, I was the first author to dedicate a book to the theory that the legendary Arthur should be identified with a historic king of Northern Britain (from Hadrian's Wall down to Lancashire and covering Yorkshire and Northumbria and Cumbria) called Arthwys ap Mar (and also recorded as Arthur Penuchel).

Pennine Dragon identified no less than 50 Arthurian characters within the circle of Arthwys ap Mar. I identified all the key Arthurian locations, from Camelot to the Lady of the Lake.

In this book I will further pinpoint Arthur's kingdom through maps and charts, as well as revealing the ancient lost books that the likes of Nennius and Geoffrey used to construct their narrative.

Was King Arthur real?

The earliest records of Arthur are consistent and give no reason to assume he was not a genuine historic leader.

In the 6th century St Gildas tells us that the Britons, after Ambrosius Aurelianus, fought a campaign against the Saxons that culminated at the Battle of Badon. A generation later one of the kings, from a Northern Dynasty, was said to have been a former charioteer to 'The Bear' which in Welsh is "Arth".

Around the same time, a scribe named Aneirin refers to a Northern warrior who fought Angles as being brave "but he was no Arthur".

Then a few hundred years later, Nennius tells us that Arthur did indeed fight the Anglo Saxons in 12 campaigns, culminating in Badon. He places him as reigning before the Northumbria based King Ida. Nennius also gives him the title 'Dux' - a rank used by the commander at Hadrian's Wall.

A date for Badon is given, again with Arthur as the leader in the Annales Cambrae. This source also lists a battle called Camlan, long identified with Camboglanna at Hadrian's Wall.

Essentially there are four sources that point towards Arthur as having been a northern leader who commanded somewhere near Hadrian's Wall. There is no reason to doubt the man existed, any more than any number of contemporary figures such as Vortigern, Ambrosius, Outigern and Maelgwyn. Indeed the evidence that Arthur existed is more persuasive than that he did not.

We then look at the king lists and find that a generation after Arthur lived, all of a sudden kings around the island were calling their sons Arthur – as if in tribute to the great man.

However we find only one man who is recorded in the king lists who could have actually been Arthur because he lived at just the right time- and that was Arthwys ap Mar, otherwise known as Arthwys of Ebrauc, Arthur Penuchel or Arthuis of the Pennines,

What do we know about King Arthur?

The earliest reference to Arthur was in the poem The Gododdin, concerning a Northern warband centred around Catterick. It was compiled in around 570AD and likens a Northern British warrior who fought Angles, to Arthur. The implication being that Arthur was also a Northern British warrior who fought the Angles – but was much more valiant.

The second reference to Arthur was in the Historia Brottonum edited by Nennius, which listed 12 battles and also gave him the title Dux Bellorum, which is comparable to the earlier title Dux Brittaniarum that was held around Hadrian's Wall.

This lists him as having won the battle of Badon, a conflict previously mentioned by Gildas as having occured after the flourit of Ambrosius and before the reigns of Maelgwyn and Cuneglas.

Of the 12 battles there is speculation as to the location, but the only ones with clear locations are in the north. Arthur is placed between the reign of Ambrosius (mid to late 5th century) and the reign in Northumbria of Ida (540s).

The next reference to Arthur is in the Annales Cambrae, where it states he fought the battle of Badon in around 516AD (possibly as early as 500) and the battle of Camlann with Mordred in around 539AD (possibly as early as 516).

Taliesin states Arthur arose around "the old renowned boundary" (certainly Hadrian's Wall) and Llywarch Hen, another northern British bard called Arthur the Guletic, a title roughly equating to a national leader or chieftain.

In later stories like Culhwch and Olwen (otherwise called Einion and Olwen), the Welsh Triads and the Saints' lives, Arthur is given various relatives including Gwenhwyfar his wife, Eigyr his mother, Uthyr (possibly his father) and warriors like Llaemenauc.He would have lived around 470-540. He is associated with the Battle of Arthuret because, although it happened after his death, Myrddin (Merlin) was present and the name is sometimes translated as Arthur's Head. He is later given the title Arthur Pendragon.

Merlin shows Vortigern the dragons

What do we know about Arthwys ap Mar?

Arthwys is recorded in several king lists which we will refer to later. Based on his family tree, we can work out that Arthwys ruled Ebrauc (York), Gododdin (Lowland Scotland down to Hadrian's Wall), Galloway, Catraeth (Catterick) and down across the Pennines. His name was probably Arthur or Artorius, and Arthwys, a regional variation.

If his grandson Peredur of York is identical with Peredur of Dumnonia or Pedr of Dyfed, he may also have been a national ruler.

He was the only ruler of his generation (he would have lived around 470-540) whose name was Arth.

It is possible he was named after Artorius Castus and, like him, commanded the 6th Legion of York.

Arthwys' son, Eleuther of York, was given the title "of the great army" and this would equate to the famous legion. He ruled the kingdom later overthrown by Ida.His brothers included Morydd, Llaenauc and Einion. His wife was Cywair, who later became a saint, and his uncle (sometimes listed as his son) was Pabo Post Prydain – father and pillar of Britain. His sons included Cinbelin, Eleuther and Keidyaw. The battle of Arthuret was fought between his and his brothers' grandsons. He is later given the title Arthur Penuchel.

Arthur Penuchel in the Northern Genealogies

The only ruler in Britain in 500AD whose name was Arth was King Arthwys ap Mar - otherwise known as Arthur Penuchel.

Ruling Ebrauc, Gododdin, Galloway, Catraeth and the Pennines, Arthwys was born in around 470AD to Mar and Gwenllian.

Arthwys was a hereditary prince in the area now known as Yorkshire, and he soon became a military leader. He was garrisoned on Hadrian's Wall and used the key military posts like Camboglanna (Camlan), Carlisle, Ebrauc and Camulod (Camelot).

He engaged the invading Angles in 12 battles across the North as Dux Bellorum, and when his father Mar died he succeeded him as king.

His uncle Pabo Post Prydain also abdicated and lived a hermit's lifestyle in Gwynedd - he was the prototypical "Merlin Emrys" and retired from fighting the Angles across the Pennines in favour of being a holy man and spiritual guide to the King.

When I published Pennine Dragon, some critics claimed that Arthur could not be Arthwys because of the different spelling. However if we re-visit the genealogies, we can see that Arthur and Arthwys were always identical:

Gwrgi a pheredur ac arthur penuchel a tonlut a hortnan a dyrnell trydyth gwyn dorliud

Gvrgi a Pheredur meibon Eliffer Gosgorduavr m Arthwys m Mar m Keneu m Coel

Gwendoleu a Nud a Chof meibyon Keidyav m Arthwys m Mar m Keneu m Coel

[C]atguallaun liu map Guitcun map Samuil pennissel map Pappo post priten map Ceneu map Gyl hen.

Dunavt a Cherwyd a Sawyl Pen Uchel meibyon Pabo Post Prydein m Arthwys m Mar m Keneu m Coel

Some of the family relationships are a little confused (Gwrdi and Pheredur go from Arthur's grandsons to his brothers, and Pabo goes from Arthur's uncle to his son), but from these genealogies we can work out a few key details.

In generation 1 we have Coel Hen, leader of Northern Britain immediately after the Romans, who as we discussed in Pennine Dragon ruled at Hadrian's Wall.

In generation 2 we have Ceneu, who along with his brother in law Cunedda, were Romano-British chieftains of the 'Vortigern generation' during the initial advent of the Saxon invasion.

In generation 3 we have Mar and his brother Pabo Post Prydein (who, in Pennine Dragon, I identified with Uther Pendragon and Ambrosius Aurelianus). We will return to Uther in another chapter.

In generation 4 we have Arthur Penuchel, otherwise known as Arthwys ap Mar, who is the Arthur Pendragon of legend.

In generation 5 we have Eliffer (Eleuther) and Keidyaw who were the sons of Arthur.

And in generation 6 we have Pheredur (Peredur) who fought the battle of Arthuret, which we know also included Myrddin (Merlin).

In a later chapter we will show where each of their kingdoms lay. Now we can look at where some of the Arthurian characters fit into history.

Main Charaters

Character: King Arthur
Historic Equivalent: Arthwys ap Mar (Arthur Penuchel)
Gildas tells us Badon was a decisive battle against the Anglo Saxons and Nennius and the Annales Cambrae tell us Arthur was the victor. Anierin's Gododdin, Nennius' battle list and the early poem Pa Gur place Arthur in the North from the Pennines, through Yorkshire and up to Hadrian's Wall. The King of this area at the time was Arthwys ap Mar. After defeating the Angles in 12 battles, he faced a rebellion from Mordred.

Character: Gwenhwyfar (Guinevere)
Historic Equivalent: Cywair
We first meet Arthur's queen Gwenhwyfar in Culhwch and Olwen. Her name means something like 'white fairy'. She is later called Guanhumura by Geoffrey and later Guinevere. She is attributed various fathers including Leodegraunce and Cywyrt. She ended her life as a nun after being abducted (by Melegaunt or Mordred). The real Gwenhwyfar was Cywair of Ireland. She may have been the daughter of king Laoghaire. She was married to Arthwys ap Mar and ended her life at Llangower with St Cywair's Church near Snowden named after her.

Character: Uther Pendragon (Iubher)
Historic Equivalent: Mar ap Ceneu
In the legends Taliesin and Pa Gur we are introduced to Uther, who boasts he contributed to Arthur's valiance. Geoffrey tells us he was Arthur's father more explicitly and his campaigns included York. His Gaelic name Iubher means Yew Tree, the same as Ebrauc. He is a love rival of Gorlois. At the time the real king of York was Mar, father of Arthwys and a nearby prince was Gorlais. While the Uther of legend succeeded his brother Ambrosius and father Constantine, Mar succeeded his brother Pabo Post Prydain and father Ceneu.

Character: Eigyr (Igrainne)
Historic Equivalent: Gwenllian

Arthur's mother, Eigyr, was the daughter of Amlawdd Gwledig and Gwen (daughter of Cunedda who was married to Coel's daughter) in stories like Culhwch - and it is through this line that Arthur has various cousins like Culhwch who is also known as Einion. The real Arthwys was also a descendant of Coel, and his mother Gwenllian is the real Eigyr. While Eigyr was the daughter of Gwen, Arthwys' mother was called Gwenllian. And while Eigyr's father was Amlawdd Gwledig, Gwenllian's father was Brychan ap Amlach Gwledig.

Character: Mordred (Medraut)
Historic Equivalent: Morydd ap Mar

We first meet Medraut in the Annales Cambrae, but then Culhwch, the Dream of Rhonabwy, Geoffrey of Monmouth and the Triads add detail that is fairly consistent. Medraut (also Modred, Mordred etc) is a relative of Arthur's (son, brother, nephew) who betrays him and leads a civil war against him at Camlan. It has been suggested that his name comes from Moderatus, a rank at Hadrian's Wall which would fit in with what we know of Arthur. The real Arthwys' brother was Morydd and this is the Mordred of legend.

Character: Llwch Llenlleawg
Historic Equivalent: Llaenauc ap Mar

Llenlleawg is one of Arthur's earliest companions in stories like Culhwch, the Spoils of Annwn and Pa Gur. He travels with Arthur to Ireland and helps rescue Gwenhwyfar. Later on, the French writers drew on this for the character Lancelot who was the son of Elaine and father of Galahad. The real Llenlleawg was Llaenauc, brother of Arthwys. His son Gwallawg is the Galahad of legend, and of course his mother Gwenllian is the legendary Elaine

Character: Myrddin Emrys (Merlin)
Historic Equivalent: Pabo Post Prydain

The character of Merlin was derived from two distinct people - The Northern British bard Myrddin Wyllt and the boy Emrys, described by Nennnius. Emrys is described as Emrys Guletic (Ambrosius the warleader) and he is equated with Ambrosius Aurelianus. According to Geoffrey this was the uncle of Arthur. In this case, he must be identified with the uncle of Arthwys ap Mar, who was Pabo Post Prydain. This warleader was known as the 'father and pillar of Britain' when he ruled the Pennines region and later became a sagely holyman in Wales. According to Geoffrey his son attended the coronation of King Arthur.

Character: Myrddin Wyllt (Merlin II)
Historic Equivalent: Myrddin

There is little mystery who this character is. Merlin's boyhood fortune-telling and later mentorship of King Arthur may be derived from King Arthur, but the majority of his traits come straight from Myrddin. Named by the Gododdin and the Annales Cambrae, Myrddin was the great great grand nephew of Arthwys and fought at the battle of Arthuret.

Contrasting King Arthur with Arthwys ap Mar

King Arthur ruled Camelot, Carduel and the City of the Legions

Arthwys ruled Camulod (Slack), Carduel (Carlisle) & Caer Legion (York)

Arthur's father was associated with York

Arthwys' father was associated with York

Arthur's wife was Gwenhwyfar ferch Cywyrt

Arthwys' wife was Cywair

Arthur's mother was Eigyr ferch Gwen

Arthwys' mother was Gwenllian

Arthur's paternal grandfather was St Constantine

Arthwys' paternal grandfather was St Ceneu

Arthur's maternal grandfather was Amlawdd Gwledig

Arthwys' maternal grandfather was Brychan ap Amlach Gwledig

Arthur's sons included Kyduan

Arthwys' sons included Cynvelyn

Arthur's nephew, brother or son was Mordred

Arthwys' brother was Morydd

Arthur's champion was Lleminawc (later Lancelot)

Arthwys' brother was Llaenauc

Lancelot's son was Galahad

Llaenauc's son was Gwallawg

Arthur's cousin was Einion (Culhwch)

Arthwys' brother was Einion

Arthur was related to Urien and Mark

Arthwys was related to Urien and Meirchionn

The earliest mention of Arthur was in 'The Gododdin' around Yorkshire

Arthwys was king in the area around The Gododdin around Yorkshire

Arthur was closely linked with Myrddin (Merlin)

Arthwys was related to Myrddin

Arthur was closely linked with Peredur

Arthwys was related to Peredur

Arthur was succeeded by the son of Cador

Arthwys was succeeded by Keidyaw

Arthur's last battle was Camlann and he was taken to Avalon

Arthwys served around Camboglanna and Avallana

Arthur was related to Morgan, Anna and Nimue

Arthwys was related to Madrun, Anna and Nyfaine

Arthur lived around 470-540

Arthwys lived around 470-540

Arthur was the Dux

Arthwys served around Hadrian's Wall, base of the Dux

Arthur was known as Pendragon

Arthwys was known as Penuchel and commanded the fort of Draco

Arthur's coronation was attended by the son of Pabo and Ceneu

Arthwys was nephew of Pabo and grandson of Ceneu

Arthur threw his sword into Vivianne's lake

Arthwys' men threw offerings to Coventina's well

Arthur was the grandfather of Cadrod Calchfynedd

Arthwys was the great grandfather of Cadrod Calchnynedd

Arthur was killed by Eda Elyn Mawr

Arthwys' kingdom was lost to Ida

Taliesin was Arthur's bard

Taliesin was from the north like Arthwys

Arthur was descended from Evdaf

Arthwys was descended from Evdaf

Arthur's 12 battles are best located in the north

Arthwys ruled the area covering the 12 battles

Mythical King Arthur Pendragon

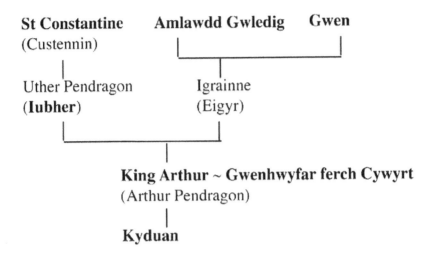

St Constantine
(Custennin)
|
Uther Pendragon
(**Iubher**)

Amlawdd Gwledig   **Gwen**

Igrainne
(Eigyr)

King Arthur ~ Gwenhwyfar ferch Cywyrt
(Arthur Pendragon)
|
Kyduan

Historic King Arthwys (Arthur Penuchel)

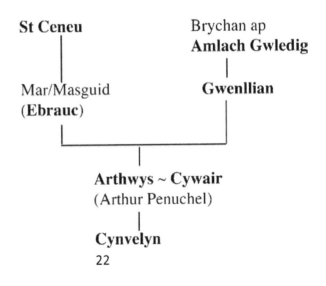

St Ceneu

Brychan ap
Amlach Gwledig

Mar/Masguid
(**Ebrauc**)

Gwenllian

Arthwys ~ Cywair
(Arthur Penuchel)
|
Cynvelyn

Artorius Castus and Arthwys

Of all the kings and leaders called Arthur, Arthwys, Athrwys and Artur, it is worth noting that the very first two served in York and Hadrian's Wall. They were Lucius Artorius Castus in the 3rd Century and Arthwys ap Mar a few hundred years later.

There are theories, notably championed by Linda Malcor, that Artorius was the basis for King Arthur. While an interesting theory, it is clear he was in the right place at the wrong time.

Almost all of the evidence for Artorius being King Arthur can more easily be applied to Arthwys, who ruled the same area but at the right time.

Lucius Artorius was not a king, but he was a general whose rulership coincides with that of the mythical Good King Lucius.

I would suggest if mythology remembers Artorius it is as King Lucius rather than as King Arthur. Interestingly, a later pedigree makes King Lucius (Lleiffer Mawer) the ancestor of Arthwys, so the name could be passed down the family. The lineage is largely mythological, including figures like Llyrd, Bran and Karadoc, who may have been inserted from an earlier mythological pedigree. But it is still interesting that our King Arthur was regarded as a descendant of King Lucius.

The pedigree from Lucius to Arthwys is:
Lleifer Mawr (Lucius the Great)
Parar
Keribir
Llyr
Bran
Karadoc
Evdaf
Cynan
Cadfan
Strawawl~Coel
Ceneu
Mar
Arthwys (King Arthur)

Lucius Artorius served in Britain, but unlike Arthur he did not die in Britain. What is known of him comes largely from inscriptions on fragments of a sarcophagus, and a memorial plaque, both found in Podstrana on the Dalmatian coast. Although undated, the likely time period of the sarcophagus (before 200), combined with the inscription's mention of Artorius being a dux, suggests that he was the unnamed commander of a 185 expedition to Armorica mentioned by Herodian. That Artorius was the Dux in the second century and his descendant Arthwys ruled the same area at the correct Arthurian time supports the idea that Arthwys too was a Dux – like the Arthur named by Nennius.

Artorius was a centurion of the Legio III Gallica, then moved to VI Ferrata, then to V Macedonica, where he was promoted to primus pilus. He was then made praepositus of the classis Misenensis (the Bay of Naples fleet), followed by a position as praefectus of the VI Victrix, which was based in Britain from 122AD. Artorius likely participated in the guarding of Hadrian's Wall.

When VI Victrix mutinied, Artorius seems to have remained loyal, since Pertinax soon after promoted him to dux and sent him to Armorica with several cohorts of cavalry, where he was successful in suppressing an uprising. Artorius then retired from the army and became procurator centenaris (governor) of Liburnia, a part of Dalmatia.

The sixth legion was founded by Octavian (the future emperor Augustus) in 41 BCE, as a copy of the Caesarian sixth legion, which was in the army of his rival Marc Antony. Perhaps veterans who had fought under Caesar joined Octavian's unit.

The legion was first deployed to Perugia, Italy and then, in 121, the emperor Hadrian visited Germania Inferior, where he ordered the construction of the Lower Rhine limes. The building activities were led by the governor, Platorius Nepos, a personal friend of Hadrian. Next year, the emperor visited Britain and took VI Victrix with him, together with Platorius, who now became governor of Britain. At the same time, VIIII Hispana came to Germania Inferior; it seems that the two legions traded places.

The soldiers of the sixth legion were now to build the British limes, which is better known as Hadrian's Wall. (They built the section between Newcastle and Carlisle, and a bridge across the river Tyne near Newcastle.) The legion's new base was York, Around 130 miles from Hadrian's Wall. This is echoed 300 years later when Arthwys commanded from York to Hadrian's Wall.

In 208, Septimius Severus came to Britain, in an attempt to conquer Scotland. VI Victrix moved to the north, where it shared a large fortress with II Augusta, at Carpow on the river Tay. During this war, it received the honorific title Britannica. From now on, the full name of the legion was VI Victrix Pia Fidelis Britannica. The conquests were abandoned at an unknown moment in the third century.

During this century, VI Victrix remained at York, and shared the fate of Britain. When this province was part of the Gallic Empire, it supported the Gallic emperors (260-274); when Britain became independent, it supported usurpers like Carausius and Allectus (286-297). After 297, the province was again incorporated in the Roman Empire, and the soldiers served crown-prince (later emperor) Constantius I Chlorus. When he died in 306 in York, soldiers of the Sixth proclaimed his son emperor: Constantine the Great (306-337).

Arthwys ap Mar followed in this tradition from Hadrian's Wall to York. Arthwys, his father Mar, his father Ceneu and his father Coel also served as the Dux, commanding what remained of the Sixth Legion, and when Arthwys died it passed to his son Eleuther who was known by the epithet 'of the great retinue'.

Where did the Dux rule?

Arthur is called the Dux Bellorum in the earliest sources. But where did the Dux rule? Fortunately we have contemporary Roman records that show this was a title used across what is now the north of England.

The Notitia Dignitatum for Britain lists several military commands (the *dux Britanniarum*, then *comes litoris Saxonici per Britannias* and the *comes Britanniarum*). They are divided up as follows:

NOTITIA DIGNITATUM OCCIDENTIS
REGISTER OF THE DIGNITARIES, CIVIL AND MILITARY, IN THE DISTRICTS OF THE WEST

Six vicars: of the Britains.
Six military counts: of the Britains; of the Saxon shore of Britain.

Twenty-two consulars:
in the Britains two:
of Maxima Caesariensis,
of Valentia.

Thirteen dukes:
… of Britannia

Thirty-one presidents:
in the Britains

COMES LITORIS SAXONICI PER BRITANNIAM
THE COUNT OF THE SAXON SHORE
Troops and Offices of the Count of the Saxon Shore

Bradwell
Dover
Lympne
Brancaster
Burgh Castle

Reculver
Richborough
Pevensey
Portchester

Sub dispositione uiri spectabilis ducis Britanniarum:
Areas of the Dux Britanniarum's command
Some places that can be identified, include:

York
Doncaster
Ilkley
South Shields

Carlisle
Drumburgh
Lancaster
Malton
Hadrian's Wall

Newcastle	Burgh-by-Sands
Chesters	Kirkbride
Carrawburgh	Bowness
Housesteads	Ravenglass
Castleheads	Lancaster
Stanwix	Ribchester

We will later see that the places governed by the Dux correspond with the 12 battle sites given by Nennius.

It is clear that the Dux Bellorum that Nennius called Arthur could only have governed in the North like the Dux described in this record.

The memory of Arthur

According to dates suggested by sources as diverse as Nennius, the Annales Cambrae and Geoffrey, Arthur must have lived around 470-540. Therefore when the Gododdin was written, in around 570 he was still in living memory. But he could also be in folk memory until at least 700AD. Many scholars would consider 700AD to be too far in history for somebody to remember a man who lived in 540AD, but this isn't the case. Grandfathers tell grandsons of their own grandfathers, and 200 years become a fairly fresh memory without the need for anything to be written down.

I know this from my own family. My maternal great great grandfather August Nilsson lived 1866-1956 and at the time of writing in 2016, my grandmother and mother still remember him well and could tell stories about him to my young children, stories they could remember for more than 50 years – 200 years after his birth. And it is not just hard facts that they remember, it is little details – how tall he was, how he mispronounced words because of his Swedish accent, how his fussy wife used to polish coal on the fire. If my great great grandfather (who never defeated a Saxon legion) can be accurately remembered after 200 years, then so could Arthur.

Even further back on the paternal side, my great great great grandfather Herve Briant (a man born in 1837 who served in Napolean III's Royal Navy) is still talked about in family folklore. He was from Brittany and his father Francois was the magistrate. He deserted his Navy post and his own father put out a warrant to have him hanged. He ended up going seal-hunting in Newfoundland and eventually came to England where he befriended a local man. The man's daughter was jilted by her fiancé and so Herve married her. Here it is not his military career that is remembered, but the rather romantic story of how he met his wife. And this, 200 years later is the first time this story has been published. So it is perfectly possible Arthur's love for his wife could be first published 200 years or so after they died.

These details are unremarkable when compared with, let's say, defeating the Saxons in 12 pitched battles, yet they live on around our family dinner tables after almost 200 years.

Human nature does not change in this way. For this reason Arthur's real memory, that of Arthur Penuchel could be carried well into the 8th century by those who knew him. There is no need for him to be confused with 2nd century Sarmatian generals, Celtic gods or comets.

People knew Arthur was a real northern warrior and he was recorded as such.

Even by the time of Nennius Arthur's life could have been a real living memory, as in the examples of my great great grandfather and great great great grandfather.

People at the time may well have known by word of mouth exactly where Arthur ruled.

Peredur is universally accepted as being a King of York (Ebrauc). He is the Sir Perceval of legend and was the grandson of Arthwys ap Mar

Arthur's Lost Grails

In later romances, Arthur goes on a quest for the Holy Grail, the cup of Christ from the Last Supper. However even in earlier Arthurian stories there are references to magic dishes, chalices and quest items. At the garrisons of Hadrian's Wall where Arthwys served there have been two notable chalices found. They were there before Arthwys but they could have been among his prized possessions.

The Dragon Cup of Camlan

Where Arthur fought his last battle at Camlan, there is an inscription on a 'grail' dedicated to the Draco (Draconis or Dragon) of Camlan. It is translated as:

Mais, Coggabata, Uxelodunum, Camboglanna, according to the line of the Aelian wall. [By the hand or The property] of Draco.

In Latin:
MAIS   COGGABATA   VXELODVNVM   CAMBOGLANNA RIGORE VALI AELI DRACONIS.

Amazingly inscribed with the names of Camlan and Draco. Picture: Dominic Coyne (Wikimedia Commons)

A cup inscribed with the name of Draco, listing Camlan and belonging to the kingdom of Arthwys, must surely be the proverbial Holy Grail of King Arthur! Of course this isn't the cup of Christ, but as Arthurian artefacts go it is a wonderful piece.

Could it be that Draco was a rank used by the commander (Dux) of the troops at Hadrian's Wall near Camboglanna? If so, our Arthur was not only Arthur Penuchel, he was also Arthur Draco. Surely the Arthur Pendragon of legend.

On the inscription Bowness (MAIS) is followed by Drumburgh-by-Sands (COGGABATA), Next comes Stanwix (VXELODVNVM), then Castlesteads (CAMBOGLANNA). These are the four of the westernmost forts on Hadrian's Wall, excluding Aballava.

Inscribed with Draco and Camlan, this bowl is truly the Holy Grail of Arthwys ap Mar. Picture: Dominic Coyne (Wikimedia Commons)

This brilliant find was discovered in 2003 by metal-detectorist Kevin Blackburn. He found the small enamelled Roman bronze cup in Staffordshire. It measures around 90mm in diameter and has a distinctly 'Celtic' style with inlaid roundels. The name Draco could refer to the tradition of Sarmatian dragon-standard bearers at Hadrian's Wall and Arthur is long associated with the Dragon banner.

It is tantalising to think that this cup could have been prized by Arthwys as the Draco of his time at Camboglanna. But this is not the only such Grail we are interested in. There is also the 'Cup of Avalon.'

"The Cup of Avalon"

Detail of the Rudge cup which names Camlan and Avalon

The Dragon cup's "twin" is the Rudge Cup, which amazingly names both our Camlan and our Avalon on the inscription. The artefact, known as the Rudge Cup, is a small enamelled bronze cup found in 1725 at Rudge, near Froxfield, in Wiltshire. The cup was found down a well on the site of a Roman villa.

It is important in that it lists five of the forts on the western section of Hadrian's Wall and two of them are of special Arthurian interest.

The information on the cup has been compared with the two major sources of information regarding forts on the Wall, the Notitia Dignitatum and the Ravenna Cosmography.

The cup is in the possession of the Duke of Northumberland and is on display at Alnwick Castle. A replica of the cup is on display at the British Museum.

As well as discovering that King Arthur was really Arthwys ap Mar, and locating the Lost Books of Arthur, it seems we have finally found two great chalices of Arthur's fortress.

They are not the Holy Grail of Christ, nor are they likely to be the cauldron that Taliesin sent Arthur looking for in the Otherworld, but they do seem to represent significant symbols for Arthur.

We have:

The Dragon Cup of Camlan: Inscribed with the name Draco and the site of Camboglanna

The Cup of Avalon: Inscribed with the names of Avalon and Camboglanna.

These are not theoretical pieces in some lost tomb. They are very real artefacts in major British museums that were in Britain at the very time Arthwys fought in those places.

Arthur in the Historia Brittonum

Ask any Arthurian scholar what the earliest historical reference to Arthur is, and they will normally answer "Nennius". However this is not entirely true nor accurate. Even if we cast aside the possibility that Arthur was alluded to by Gildas, Anierin, Taliesin, Llywarch Hen and so on, naming the author of the Historia Brittonum as Nennius is not entirely true either.

There are a number of surviving manuscripts of the Historia. Some name Nennius as the author – or at least the editor – and some do not. But the earliest manuscript that survived into the 20th century listed the author as Filius Urbagen (son of Urien), this son of Urien, while possibly referring to Owain, is more likely to refer to Rhun ap Urien.

This is hugely significant in the hypothesis that Arthwys was Arthur. Because Urien's grandfather served with Arthwys, they were cousins and Urien was on the same side as Arthwys' grandson Peredur. Therefore it makes perfect sense that the Arthur of the Historia was Arthwys.

Unfortunately this manuscript was destroyed in the Second World War! This is our Lost Book of Arthur and unfortunately a German bomb meant it cannot be found (the Saxons had the last laugh). But fortunately we do have a record of it and it is still recorded at the British Library as the Chartres Manuscript.

The great Arthurian author EWB Nicholson recorded at the turn of the century:

A 100+ year old record of the manuscript before it was destroyed:

I hold:
I)   that the Chartres MS contains not Nennius but a work which is one of the sources of Nennius.
II)   That this work is itself a compilation
III)   That it was written in the territory of the Northern Kymri
IV)   That the latest part of it is not earlier than 752

*V)   That the earliest part may have been compiled by Tun the
son of Urbgen, from whom Nennius states that the Northmbrians
received baptism*

*VI)   That the Urbgen in question may be the British king
mentioned by Nennius*

*VII)   The MS does not contain anywhere the name of Nennius,
or that of any of the persons named by Nennius as his
instructors...*

*Except that like Nennius, it introduces the miracles of Germanus
by the words 'aliquanta miracula quae per illum fecit dominus
scribenda decreui, it lacks all Nennius's personal notes. And it
lacks all his references to prae-existing documents...*

*It states that what is about to follow is discovered from **Old
Books from our Old authors**, that is of much earlier British
writers, and I hold that the Chartres text represents the actual
source of the discovery.*

VIII)

*IX)   The title of the Chartres text (as far as it can be
reoresented without special type) is as follows:*

X)

*XI)   INCIPIUNT – EXBERTA – FILU URBAGEN DE LIBRI
SCI GERMANI – INUENTA & ORIGINE & GENELOGIA
BRITONY*

*The archetype, in fact, was professedly a collection of excerpts
such as Nennius himself speaks of. The first of these excerpts was
**The son of Urbagen's discoveries relating to the Book of St
Germanus and the origin and genealogy of the Britons...***

*The evidence that this particular collection was made in the
territory of the Northern Kymri lies in the interpolation
respecting the date of the Saxon invasion in Britain...*

*Zimmer (Nennius Vindicatus) has already argued that our
Historia Britonum is partly based on a North Kymric chronicle of*

679 which received additions down to the period 737-758...

There is little doubt that the person who mentions it was a Briton... He probably wrote in Alclyde or Carlile...

The reasons for identifying Filius Urbagen with Run Map Urbgen, and for identifying his father with the British King Urbgen, are these. The name Urbgen is of extreme rarity in Britain – so rare that I doubt there being any authentic instance of it except in the case of King Urbgen. And the presence of the connecting vowel in Urbagen is evidence that the person alluded to lived at least prior to 731...

Had the Chartres manuscript of the Historia Brittonum not been destroyed in the 1940s, it might now be seen as the definitive Historia, and Rhun ap Urien might be by many Arthurian authors of the last 70 years be viewed as the author, and Nennius only as a later editor.

In this book I will argue that Rhun ap Urien was the author of what I term 'The Lost Book of Arthur' which comprises in part the text that was used in the Chartres Historia Brittonum and later edited by Nennius.

Rhun was in essence, the man who recorded Arthur's history and he was a man whose grandfather fought alongside Arthur in the north of Britain.

The Historia Brittonum gives us 12 battles for Arthur, four of which were fought at the same location – so really he gives us 9 locations to work from.

In Pennine Dragon I described the locations of these battles as being in the North. They are as follows:

- Dubglas – the River Douglas in Wigan
- Tribruit – the River Ribble in Preston
- Badon – Batham in Buxton
- Glein – in Northumberland
- Celidon in Scotland
- Guinnion in Durham

- Agned in Edinburgh
- Bassas in Glasgow or Cumbria
- The City of the Legions – York or Chester

We should point out that in a later version of the Historia, there is an annotation (known as a gloss) which calls Arthur: "Arthur mab uter britannice, filius horribilis Latine; quoniam a pueritia sua crudelis fuit" normally translated as "Arthur terrible son, since he was particularly horrible even in childhood." However this line has caused some to assume that Geoffrey based his Uther Pendragon (or that Arthur was Arthur ap Uther) on the simple line "Arthur mab Uter".

However, as I pointed out in Pennine Dragon, not only does the character of Uther predate Geoffrey's work – he was always associated with Arthur and indeed as a relative. Uther even talks about having contributed to Arthur's valour.

The name Uther does not come from Uter (terrible) it is actually derived from Iubher (Ebrauc) the old Roman name for York. We should also observe Arthwys had a son called Eleuther – a possible throwback.

Nennius must have been working from an older source that lists Arthur's first 11 battles. Even if this were a song, nursery rhyme or poem. One could argue he got the Badon reference from Gildas, but that still doesn't explain where Nennius got battles like Dubglas and Glein from. It is now clear that the original author was in plain sight all along where Rhun is listed as the author. Nennius was merely a later editor.

This now forgotten source is what we will refer to as **The Lost Book of Arthur** and the author was Rhun ap Urien.

The Annales Cambrae and Geoffrey

The Annales Cambrae contains reference to Badon (also seen in Gildas and Nennius). Like Nennius, it links Arthur to the battle. But unlike Nennius it misses out 11 other battles but includes Camlann.

The Annales Cambrae therefore must have a different source to Nennius and Gildas. It also does not mention Ambrosius Aurelianus (unless he is identical with Pabo whom it does mention) which again, suggests the source for the Annales is not Nennius or Gildas.

So if Gildas was our first source, Aneirin our second source, Taliesin our third source and Rhun our fourth source, we now understand that since none of these mention Mordred or Camlan, there must have been a fifth source.

We will refer to the source containing the Camlan entry as **The Lost Book of Mordred.**

The Annales also include reference to the battle of Arthuret and the note about Myrddin. Geoffrey of Monmouth also has a version of the Arthuret story, but much more besides. This comes from the source we will refer to as **The Lost Book of Uther.**

Much of the Arthurian legend can be traced to Geoffrey of Monmouth's History of the Kings of Britain. It is clear that Geoffrey also must have had access to The Lost Book of Uther. He includes information on Arthwys, Peredur, Eleuther and Uther that could only have come from a lost Northern Chronicle. Geoffrey himself tells us:

Walter, archdeacon of Oxford, a man of great eloquence, and learned in foreign histories, offered me a very ancient book in the British tongue.

This 'very ancient book in the British tongue' is what I will refer to, for the sake of simplicity, as **The Lost Book of Uther.**

This book was alluded to by Gerald of Wales (Giraldus) in his Descriptio Cambriae.

Giraldus referred to books, subsequently destroyed, 'quos de gestis Arthuri. et gentis suae laudibus multos [Gildas] scripserat.'

The story went that Arthur's adventures were actually recorded by Gildas but then an unfortunate incident unfolded. Arthur was, for some reason, in disguise and was strutting his stuff on the dancefloor of a banquet hall. Gildas' brother Hueill decided to blow Arthur's cover based on a leg injury he had. Arthur dragged Hueill into the street, lay Hueill's head on a stone and with a mighty stroke of Excalibur decapitated him. The stone, which of course has an Excalibur shaped dent, is now in Ruthin town centre with a bank built next to it. Gildas of course was aggrieved by his brother's death and so destroyed his books about Arthur.

It seems likely that this is an apocryphal story to justify Gildas not mentioning Arthur (and possibly to create a nice Welsh legend about an odd stone) but it is another example of a 'Lost Book of Arthur.'

PART TWO

THE KINGS OF BRITAIN

The Kings and Emperors of Britain

Britain was part of the Roman Empire for some 400 years – almost from the time of Christ to the start of the 5th century to simplify.

In the decline of Rome, British (Celtic) tribes once headed by a Roman commander such as the Votadini began to emerge as client kingdoms in their own right and naturally, when Rome departed, the once generals became de facto kings of the region.

As the historian Procopius later explained, "from that time onwards it remained under [the rule] of tyrants."

Roman Emperors of Britain including usurpers

Constantius (305-306)
Constantine I (306-337)
Constantine II (337-340)
Constans (337-350)
Octavius (350-383 conjectural)
Magnus Maximus (383-388)
Eugenius (392-394)
Marcus (406)
Gratian (407)
Constantine III (407-411)

In 402 the Emperor Stilicho faced wars with the Visigoth king Alaric and the Ostrogoth king Radagaisus. He naturally summoned troops, including those at the very northern frontiers of the Empire – Hadrian's Wall.

402 is also the last date of any Roman coinage found in large numbers in Britain, suggesting either that Stilicho also stripped the remaining troops from Britain, or that the Empire could no longer afford to pay the troops. It is, in a sense, the dawn of the Dark Ages.

Meanwhile, the Picts (north of the wall), Saxons and other Germanic peoples and Scoti (from Ireland) continued their raids, since Britain was no longer as protected.

In 405, for example, Niall of the Nine Hostages is described as having raided along the southern coast of Britain. We will return to Niall later in the chapter.

The rise of the Gododdin

First recorded as the Otadinoi, this Iron Age Celtic tribe occupied the eastern coastal section of modern southern Scotland and north-eastern England, from the Firth of Forth down as far as the border with the Brigantes. They essentially occupied the area close to Hadrian's Wall.

The name Otadinoi, or Votadini, has its etymology in the Indo-European name for 'stand' in the sense of foundation or support. They may have had an ancestor called Votad or Wotad – or possibly it is related to the Germanic deity Wotan (Odin).

It is thought that the Northern HQ of the Votadini was Edinburgh, where a hill fort called Traprain Law stood on what is now called Arthur's Seat.

Among the earliest Gododdin chieftains of note is Cunedda. His genealogy is as follows:

Tacit (Tacitus)
Paternus
Edern (*Æturnus*)
Cunedda (Cunodagos)

Cunedda's grandfather Paternus is recorded in Welsh folklore as Padarn Beisrudd, which literally translates as Paternus of the "red tunic" which suggests a High Roman rank. Looking at the Roman style names in the lineage it may be that Cunedda was not a native Votadini, but rather from a Roman family put in military control of men drawn from a Votadini warband.

Interestingly, in later genealogies Cunedda is considered a great grandfather of King Arthur (Arthur's mother Eigyr was the daughter of Gwen who was said to be Cunedda's daughter).

Mythological pedigree of Arthur from Coel and Cunedda:

Coel ~ Stradwawl
Gwawl ~ Cunedda
Gwen ~ Amlawdd
Eigyr ~ Uther
Arthur

Historic pedigree of Arthwys from Coel:

Coel ~ Stradwawl
Ceneu
Mar ~ Gwenllian
Arthwys

Paternus would have likely served an Emperor such as Magnus Maximus and we should note that both Maximus and Cunedda are later given the title Gwledig.

Folklore has Cunedda marrying Gwawl, whose father was Coel Hen Guotepauc. Although the name Gwawl may be contrived from [Hadrian's] Wall, this dynastic marriage makes perfect sense as Coel was ruler in the neighbouring kingdom, which stretched down from the southern Votadini border across what is now Yorkshire.

Again we see that King Arthur's legendary pedigree was rooted in the mythology of Hadrian's Wall from Coel to Stradwawl, to Gwawl.

Coel's genealogy is as follows:

Teuhvant
Tegfan
[Guatepauc]
Coel Hen Gautepauc

Coel's wife is listed as Stradwawl (again related to the Wall) and she is given a Romanised genealogy whereby her grandfather Cynan (Conanus) was the son of Evdaf (Octavius) who was said to be the father-in-law of Magnus Maximus.

The sons of Cunedda were said to have founded kingdoms in North Wales. It is likely they were sent there to repel Irish invaders.

His sons included Einion Yrth, who inherited control over the newly-founded kingdom of Gwynedd, aided by his brother Ceredig, ruler of Ceredigion, and his nephew Meirion, ruler of Meirionnydd.

Einion Yrth was of the generation of Arthur's father. Indeed, in Pennine Dragon, I suggested that Einion and his son Cadwallon Lawhir could have been the origin of Ector and his son Cai Hir (Sir Kay) who were Arthur's foster father and brother.

We will now break down every generation from Coel (generation 1), to Cunedda and Vortigern (generation 2), to the generation occupied by Ambrosius and Uther (generation 3) to the time of Arthur (generation 4), to the time of the tyrants decried by Gildas (generation 5), to the time of men like Peredur (generation 6), to the generation occupied by the later Arthur of Dyfed and Artur of Dalriada (generation 7), to the time of Meurig (generation 8) to the time of Athrwys ap Meurig (generation 9). Of course Arthwys ap Mar is the only Arthur found in generation 4.

Generation 1 & 2 (Vortigern's generation) C410-450AD

Coel Hen Vortepauc: Northern Britain and Gododdin
Agricola: Dyfed (may be identical with Coel Hen)
Cunedda: Gododdin, later Gwynedd
Ceneu: Northern Britain
Vortigern: Possibly derived from a number of leaders with this title including Coel, Cunedda, Ceneu and the Irish Fortchern.
Garbaniawn: Southern Gododdin

Saxons:

Hengist: Unknown, possibly Kent
Horssa: Unknown

I have included Generation 1 and 2 as interchangeable. Coel's epithet (the old) suggests he spanned at least two generations. It is also possible he is identical with Air-Coll (Agricola) of Dyfed and may be the Coll alluded to at Tintagel on the stone "Artognou descendant of Coll". It is also possible that Coel's son Ceneu and his son-in-law Cunedda are memories of the same person. Similarly it is possible that Coel Guatepauc (the same word as Vortipor) was related to Vortigern. Coel may have even been Vortigern the Elder. We should note that Vortigern Vorteneu has similar exploits to Ceneu, as does Cunedda.

In my opinion Cunedda was a Romanised general who served Coel, and Ceneu was the son of Coel who came to be known as Vortigern.

What we do know is that Coel was the strongest ruler in Northern Britain - possibly all of Britain - when the Romans left and he contended with invasions from Ireland.

Did Coel (as Agricola) conquer the Irish in Dyfed? We know that the Irish king at the time was a strong ruler named Niall who led excursions into Britain.

It is interesting that Ceneu was renowned as a king in the north but a saint in Dyfed. After his kingship he was recorded as an early bishop of Menevia (St Davids).

He established a church or monastic community (clas) at the site of the current settlement of Clydau which was long known as Llangeneu in his honour.

Gildas records the foolish tyrant inviting the Saxons to Britain as follows. We should note it was "to repel the invasions of the northern nations."

Then all the councillors, together with that proud tyrant, the British king, were so blinded, that, as a protection to their country, they sealed its doom by inviting in among them (like wolves into the sheep-fold), the fierce and impious Saxons, a race hateful both to God and men, to repel the invasions of the northern nations. Nothing was ever so pernicious to our country, nothing was ever so unlucky. What palpable darkness must have enveloped their minds - darkness desperate and cruel! Those very people whom, when absent, they dreaded more than death itself, were invited to reside, as one may say, under the selfsame roof. Foolish are the princes, as it is said, of Thafneos, giving counsel to unwise Pharaoh. A multitude of whelps came forth from the lair of this barbaric lioness, in three cyuls, as they call them, that is, in three ships of war, with their sails wafted by the wind and with omens and prophecies favourable, for it was foretold by a certain soothsayer among them, that they should occupy the country to which they were sailing three hundred years, and half of that time, a hundred and fifty years, should plunder and despoil the same. They first landed on the eastern side of the island, by the invitation of the unlucky king, and there fixed their sharp talons, apparently to fight in favour of the island, but alas! more truly against it. Their mother-land, finding her first brood thus successful, sends forth a larger company of her wolfish offspring, which sailing over, join themselves to their bastard-born comrades. From that time the germ of iniquity and the root of contention planted their poison amongst us, as we deserved, and shot forth into leaves and branches. The barbarians being thus introduced as soldiers into the island, to encounter, as they falsely said, any dangers in defence of their hospitable entertainers, obtain an allowance of provisions, which, for some time being plentifully bestowed, stopped their doggish mouths. Yet they complain that their monthly supplies are not furnished in sufficient abundance, and they industriously aggravate each occasion of quarrel, saying that unless more liberality is shown them, they will break the treaty and plunder the whole island. In a short time, they follow up their threats with deeds.

While Coel and Ceneu ruled supreme in Britain, their counterpart in Ireland was Niall of the Nine Hostages. This name came from the fact that king Niall abducted the young sons of nine regional kings. He used this as a bargaining tool. When it is said that the

Britons invited the Saxons as mercenaries to fight Irish invasion, it is probably Niall they are referring to!

Niall Noigiallach was the son of Eochaid Mugmedón and both he and his father were among the great high kings of Ireland. Niall was the only son of Eochaid and his wife Catharann, daughter of an English king. Eochaid later married Mong-Fionn, daughter of the king of Munster, and had another four sons. These sons were Brian, Fiachra, Ailill and Fergus.

It is said that Mong-Fionn was jealous of her stepson Niall; she wanted Brian to succeed to Eochaid. She did not rest until she had Niall as an outcast and his mother reduced down to servant.

As Niall was entering manhood, he was returned to the court and welcomed by his father. One of his first acts was to restore his mother to her rightful place. Niall underwent many tests and excelled on every one.

Niall's stepmother still had her hopes for Brian and upon Eochaid's death, she managed to get her brother kingship until Brian came of age. Once in power, however, Crimthann betrayed his sister and took full control of the kingdom instead of regency. To Crimthann's credit, he proved to be a strong king and ruled for twenty years.

During his early reign, Niall consolidated his power and home by subduing his enemies and taking hostages from the families in opposition. Meanwhile the Picts were getting wary of the small Irish colony of Dalriada which is now Scotland. They attacked and severely damaged the colony. In response Niall ventured to Scotia Minor and the land of the Picts, here again subduing all and gaining submission through the taking of royal hostages – hence the name, Niall of the Nine Hostages.

After a short consolidation, he marched south with his Scot and Pict allies against the Romans in Britain. It was there that Niall's forces took hostage one Succat, who is better known by his later name of St. Patrick. Besides taking St. Patrick in his youth, Niall is known mainly for two things. First, he consolidated the northern region of Ireland and created a dynasty that kept his descendants High Kings of Ireland for six hundred years. Second, his military ability led him to the Irish taking control of all of Alba and a large part of Britain.

Niall was the father of a great many Irish clans and DNA testing has shown he liked to spread his royal seed! One of his sons was Maine Mor, the founder of the Ui Maine clan. Interestingly in one legend Uther has relatives called (or variously spelled) Ivoire, Ivoine, Moine or Maine. This king Maine was succeeded by Breasal, he by Dallan, he by Lusach, he by Fearach and he by the great Cairbre Crom who went on to become high king of Munster. Cairbre Crom is of particular interest to the author because he was the ancestor of the Clann MacAodhagain (Clan Keegan) and my 39x great grandfather.

I believe the adventures of Niall into Britain, and Britain's defences against the Irish leading to the invitation of the Saxons are absolutely key to understanding this generation. Niall's involvement in Arthurian affairs should be researched further.

Generation 1 & 2
The Vortigern Generation
C410-450AD

Note: Ceneu may be identical with Vortigern Vortineu. Agricola may be identical with Coel.

Generation 3 (Uther Pendragon's generation)c450-490

Pabo Post Prydain: Pennines
Mar: Ebrauc, Gododdin, Galloway
Fergus Mor: Dal Riada May be identical with Mar
Ambrosius Aurelianus: Unknown, may be identical with Pabo
Dumnagual Moilmut: Clyde
Dyfnwal Hen: Strathclyde (may be identified with Dumnagual)
Gurgust: Rheged
Einion Yrth: Gwynedd
Pebiau: Ergyng
Erbin: Kernow
Erbin: Dyfed (may be identical with Erbin of Kernow)
Erbin: Strathclyde (may be identical with Erbin of Kernow & Dyfed)
Riothamus: Unknown, possibly Britanny

Saxons

Aesc: Unknown, possibly Kent

In Pennine Dragon, I argued that Ambrosius Aurelianus (uncle of King Arthur in mythology) should be identified with Pabo Post Prydain (uncle of Arthwys). In this generation there was also a notable historic king named Riothamus who has been identified with not only Ambrosius and Uther but also Arthur. We will discuss Riothamus later.

In Geoffrey of Monmouth, the emperor Constantine was succeeded by his sons Ambrosius and Uther and they by Arthur. In reality we know the northern-based ruler Ceneu was succeeded by his sons Pabo and Mar, and they by Arthwys.

It is also interesting to note that at the time Mar/Mor was ruling in the north, the ruler in Scotland was Fergus Mor. Is it possible that Mar was actually a mercenary from the north named Fergus Mor who was employed by Ceneu rather than being his son?

Leaving Ambrosius and Uther (and Pabo, Mar and Fergus Mor) alone, there are other rulers in this generation worth our attention. Another interesting anomaly is Erbin – kings in Strathclyde, Dumnonia and Dyfed were recorded as being called Erbin in this generation, and each were recorded as being followed by somebody called Gereint (or a similar variation).

It is possible that Pabo (for example) was considered emperor and Mar his Dux and Erbin his Commes. This would explain why they are found in various locations throughout the country.

We find, for example, Mar-Uther in Dumnonia as Morvawr.

Riothamus

In Pennine Dragon I argued that King Uther-Mor and his brother King Pabo could have led excursions to Britanny where they became known as Ri-Otha-Mus and Riwal-Pabo. Regardless of whether Riothamus and Riwal were native British kings like Mar and Pabo, or whether they came from a different dynasty, Riothamus is a notable king and listed in contemporary history.

The Gothic historian Jordane's the "Gothic History" included a request made to the Britons, by the Roman Emperor Anthemius, for help in battling the Visigoths. The British responded by sending Riothamus and 12,000 men to the aid of Rome.

The text is as follows:

Now Euric, king of the Visigoths, perceived the frequent change of Roman Emperors and strove to hold Gaul by his own right. The Emperor Anthemius heard of it and asked the Brittones for aid. Their King Riotimus came with twelve thousand men into the state of the Bituriges by the way of Ocean, and was received as he disembarked from his ships.

Euric, king of the Visigoths, came against them with an innumerable army, and after a long fight he routed Riotimus, king of the Brittones, before the Romans could join him. So when he had lost a great part of his army, he fled with all the men he could gather together, and came to the Burgundians, a neighboring tribe then allied to the Romans. But Euric, king of the Visigoths, seized the Gallic city of Arverna; for the Emperor Anthemius was now dead.

Generation 3
The Uther Generation
C450-490

Note: The Erbin in Dumnonia may refer to Erbin in Scotland (Damnonia). Mar, ruler of York (Ebrauc) is the best candidate for Uther Pendragon who fought campaigns in York. Pabo and Pebiau probably different. Mar may be identical with Fergus Mor.

Generation 4 (King Arthur's generation) c490-540

Arthwys: Ebrauc, Gododdin, Galloway, Pennines, Catraeth
Domangart: Dal Riada (may be identical with Arthwys)
Gereint: Kernow
Vortipor or Guartepir: Dyfed (may be Gereint)
Gereint: Strathclyde (Gereint of Kernow?)
King Arthur: Identified with Arthwys
Bran Hen: Clyde
Merchiaun: Rheged
Llaenauc: Elmet
Samyl: Pennines
Cadwallon Lawhir: Gwynedd
Owain Ddantgwyn: Rhos
Cadell: Powys
Cynfyn: Ergyng
Clydno: Galloway

Saxons:

Octha: Unknown, possibly Kent
Aelle: Unknown, possibly Sussex
Cerdic: Wessex, may have been Romano British Dux Gewissae

If Coel was the country's over king in Generation 1, his son Ceneu in Generation 2, his sons Pabo and Mar in generation 3, we find to little surprise it is Mar's son Arthwys in generation 4.

Nominally the King of Ebrauc, the genealogies suggest he was also the ruler of Gododdin, Galloway, Catraeth and the Pennines – in other words the entire north. And just as **Art**hwys succeeded **Mor** in Ebrauc, in Dalriada it is recorded that Domang**art** succeeded Fergus **Mor**.

And much as Arthwys was famously a descendant of Coel, the Tintagel stone records a Kernow ruler as Artognou, descendant of Coll.

The author with the Artognou Stone at Tintagel Castle.

Much as in the Arthurian legends there was the warrior Gereint, in this generation we find Gereint in Dumnonia, Gereint in Strathclyde and Guartepir in Dyfed.

If Arthur was the Dux it seems that Gereint was a senior ranking officer.

In Pennine Dragon I identified a number of Arthwys' contemporaries with their Arthurian counterparts, including:

Bran Hen: King Ban
Merchiaun: King Mark
Llaenauc: Lleminawc (later Sir Lancelot)
Cadwallon Lawhir: Cai Hir (later Sir Kay)
Owain Ddantgwyn: Bedwyr (later Sir Bedevere)

The reign of Arthwys fits in seamlessly with the reign of Arthur. Both ruled in generation 4, succeeding the Ambrosius generation.

After the death of Arthwys, his kingdom was carved up among his sons:

Eleuther: Ebrauc
Cinbelin: Gododdin
Keidyaw: Galloway (possibly identical with Cador of Dumnonia, Congair of Dyfed)
Greidol: Unknown

It seems that Keidyaw (Sir Cador) was the preferred son in terms of inheritance, whereas Eleuther (Llacheu, Sir Loholt) took the 'great retinue' that was the 6th Legion. Whereas Cinbelin (Kyduan) – who I identified with Amhar in Pennine Dragon – took the Gododdin. In Arthurian legends Llacheu, Amhar and Gwydre pre-deceased their father and so Arthur passed his kingdom to Constantine who was the son of Cador.

Owain Ddantgwyn

Owain was suggested as the real King Arthur by Graham Phillips, based largely on Gildas calling his son Cuneglas, a bear (bear is Arth), and therefore suggesting it was a family name. Owain did live at the right time to be Arthur - indeed in Pennine Dragon I suggested he could have been Arthur's loyal friend Bedwyr – but, this aside, the evidence is flimsy. Gildas also says Cuneglas has a sword "special to himself" which could of course have been a special sword handed down by his "bear" father. However these arguments also hinge on Owain having been king of the huge kingdom of Powys – which he probably was not. It also hinges on Gildas meaning Owain when he mentioned the Bear. If we were to go back to 500AD, there was indeed a North Welsh king called Owain Ddantgwyn – but there was also a king in York called Arthwys – it defies belief that Arthur was the former rather than the latter. In fact Arthwys and Owain were cousins. Owain's grandmother was Gwawl, and Arthwys' grandfather was her brother Ceneu – they were the son and daughter of Coel Hen.

Even if it were proven Owain was at Badon, he still could have been so under the command of Arthwys.

Arthwys ap Mar is recorded in the king lists as an historic ruler, in descent from Coel Hen. The existence of Arthwys is not in question. From the lineages we understand that he ruled northern Britain in circa 500AD. Furthermore, Arthwys should be identified with the 'Arthur Penuchel' associated with the kings of Ebrauc.

This Arthwys, or Arthur Penuchel, lived at precisely the right time to be identified with the legendary King Arthur. The places most associated with Arthur can be located within the kingdom of Arthwys. For example:

Camlann - Camboglanna on Hadrian's Wall
    Avalon - Avallana on Hadrian's Wall
    Badon - Bardon on Hadrian's Wall
    Vivianne's Lake - Coventina's Well on Hadrian's Wall
    Carduel - Carlisle on Hadrian's Wall
    Camelot - Camulod - Slack near Huddersfield

The people most associated with Arthur can be found in the family tree of Arthwys. For example:

    Arthur – Arthwys
    Gwenhwyfar - Arthwys' wife Cywair
    Mordred - Arthwys' brother Morydd
    Einion (Culhwch) - Arthwys' brother Einion
    Lleminawc - Arthwys' brother Llaenauc
    Galahad - Arthwys' nephew Gwallawg
    Peredur - Arthwys' grandson Peredur
    Cador - Arthwys' son Keidyaw
    Myrddin - Arthwys's brother's grandson Myrddin

Generation 4
The Arthur Generation
C490-540

Note: Vortipor (Guartipor) may be identified with Gereint. Arthwys and Domangart may be identical. Gereint ap Erbin in Dumnonia may not have existed and could have been confused with Gereint ap Erbin in Scotland (or vice versa). Arthwys is also listed as Arthur Penuchel, and is the only serious candidate for King Arthur.

Generation 5 (Gildas Generation) C540-570

Eleuther: Ebrauc & Catraeth
Outigern (possibly identical with Eleuther): Bryneich
Cinbelin: Gododdin
Keidyaw: Galloway
Gwallawg: Elmet
Dunaut: Pennines
Morcant Bulc: Clyde
Cinmarc: Rheged
Dobunni: Aurelius Caninus
Constantine: Dumnonia or Damnonia
Cador: Dumnonia (may be identical with Keidyaw of Ebrauc)
Cyngar: Dyfed (may be identical with Keidyaw of Ebrauc or Cador)
Comgal: Dal Riada
Gabran: Dal Riada
Maelgwyn: Gwynedd
Cuneglas: Powys or Rhos
Gwrgan Mawr: Ergyng
Tutagual: Strathclyde

Saxons:

Eormenric: Kent
Aescwine: Essex
Ida: Bernicia
Cynric: Wessex

An excellent source for this generation is Gildas, who names Maelgwyn, Constantine, Aurelius Caninus, Cuneglas and Vortepor:

Britain has kings, but they are tyrants; she has judges, but unrighteous ones; generally engaged in plunder and rapine, but always preying on the innocent; whenever they exert themselves to avenge or protect, it is sure to be in favour of robbers and criminals; they have an abundance of wives, yet are they addicted to fornication and adultery; they are ever ready to take oaths, and as often perjure themselves; they make a vow and almost immediately act falsely; they make war, but their wars are against their countrymen, and are unjust ones; they rigorously prosecute thieves throughout their country, but those who sit at table with them are robbers, and they not only cherish but reward them; they give alms plentifully, but in contrast to this is a whole pile of crimes which they have committed; they sit on the seat of justice, but rarely seek for the rule of right judgment; they despise the innocent and the humble, but seize every occasion of exalting to the utmost the bloody-minded; the proud, murderers, the combined and adulterers, enemies of God, who ought to be utterly destroyed and their names forgotten.

And thou too, Cuneglasse, why art thou fallen into the filth of thy former naughtiness, yea, since the very first spring of thy tender youth, thou bear, thou rider and ruler of many, and guider of the chariot which is the receptacle of the bear, thou contemner of God, and vilifier of his order, thou tawny butcher, as in the Latin tongue thy name signifies. Why dost thou raise so great a war as well against men as also against God himself, against men, yea, thy own countrymen, with thy deadly weapons, and against God with thine infinite offences? Why, besides thine other innumerable backslidings, having thrown out of doors thy wife, dost thou, in the lust, or rather stupidity of thy mind, against the apostle's express prohibition, denouncing that no adulterers can be partakers of the kingdom of heaven, esteem her detestable sister, who had vowed unto God the everlasting contineney, as the very dower (in the language of the poet) of the celestial nymphs? Why cost thou provoke with thy frequent injuries the lamentations and sighs of saints, by thy means corporally afflicted, which will in time to come, like a fierce lioness, break thy bones in pieces? Desist, I beseech thee (as the prophet saith) from wrath, and leave off thy deadly fury, which thou breathest out against heaven and earth, against God and his flock, and which in time will be thy own torment; rather with altered mind obtain the prayers of those who possess a power of binding over this world, when in this world they bind the guilty, and of loosing when they loose the penitent. Be not (as the apostle saith) proudly wise, nor hope thou in the uncertainty of riches, but in God who giveth thee many things abundantly, and by the amendment of thy manners purchase unto thyself a good foundation for hereafter, and seek to enter into that real and true state of existence which will be not transitory but everlasting. Otherwise, thou shalt know and see, yea, in this very world, how bad and bitter a thing it is for thee to leave the Lord thy God, and not have his fear before thine eyes, and in the next, how thou shalt be burned in the foul encompassing flames of endless fire, nor yet by any manner of means shalt ever die. For the souls of the sinful are as eternal in perpetual fire, as the souls of the just in perpetual joy and gladness.

Generation 5
The Gildas Generation
C540-580

Comgall &
Gabran

Morcant

Tutagual   Cinbelin

Outigern

Keidyaw

Cinmarc

Dunaut   Ida

ELEUTHER

Gwallawg

Maelgwyn   Cuneglas

Gwrgan

Aurelius
Cyngar   Conan

Eormenric

Cador &   Cynric   Aescwine
Constantine

Note: Cyngar of Dyfed, Cador of Dumnonia and Keidyaw may be identical. Eleuther may be identical with Outigern.

Generation 6 (Peredur's Generation) C560-600

Peredur: Ebrauc
Peredur: Kernow (may be Peredur of Ebrauc)
Pedr: Dyfed (may be Peredur of Ebrauc & Kernow)
Coledauc: Clyde
Urien: Northern Rheged
Llywarch Hen: Southern Rheged
Gurci: Catraeth
Cynwyd: Gododdin, moving to Calchfynedd
Ceretic: Elmet
Gwendollau: Galloway
Rhun: Gwynedd
Cyngen: Powys or Rhos
Caradoc Vreichvras: Ergyng
Rhydderch Hen: Strathclyde
Aedan: Dal Riada

Saxons:

Athelbert: Kent
Sledda: Essex
Uffa: East Angles
Creoda: Mercia
Glappa and Atha: Bernicia
Ceawlin: Wessex
Cutha: Wessex (Romano British?)

This generation, the generation of Arthur's grandsons, fought for power at the aptly named Arthuret.

The traditional site of the battle at Arthuret is less than 20 miles from Birdoswald Roman fort and Camlann.

When I visited Birdoswald I observed two successive massive timber halls on the site of the north granary, which would be consistent with occupation by a local ruler with control of substantial resources. The halls cannot be precisely dated but the date given is 520 – which shows it was a post Roman site and used in the flourish of Arthur. Could it have been Arthur's base for Camlann and then his son's base for Arthuret?

As we will see in the subsequent chapter, Hadrian's Wall was Arthur's key outpost. Yes he may have fought as far north as Edinburgh and as far south as Chester, but the hub of his battles was along the wall.

The mainline lineage of Arthwys shows the strongest kings who were based at Ebrauc and commanded Hadrian's Wall:

Kings of Ebrauc

> Coel Hen (Generation 1)
> Ceneu (Generation 2)
> Mar (Generation 3)
> Arthwys (Generation 4)
> Eleuther (Generation 5)
> Peredur (Generation 6)

Generation 6
The Peredur Generation
C580-600

Note: Peredur of Dumnonia, Pedr of Dyfed and Peredur of York may be identical. Aedan of Dalriada is the father of Artur.

Generation 7: (Arthur II generation)C580-640

Owen: Rheged
Tewdwr: Dumnonia or Kernow
Tewdrig: Gwent (may be identical with Tewdwr of Dumnonia)
Arthur II: Dyfed
Beli: Gwynedd
Brochfael: Powys
Caurdaf: Ergyng
Nechtan: Strathclyde
Eochaid (note, brother of Arthur of Dal Riada)

Saxons:

Eadbald: Kent
Saebert: Essex
Tylila: East Angles
Pyda: Mercia
Athelfrith: Northumbria
Cuthwine: Wessex
Ceol: Wessex (Romano British?)

Arthur ap Pedr was born 90 years too late to be the real King Arthur, however succeeding Retheior (Pedr) and Eleuther – he did succeed two men whose names were similar to Uther, and they in turn succeeded Congair – similar to Constantine. Thus, despite having identified Arthwys ap Mar with King Arthur, it is certain that later chronicles confused his genealogy with that of his great grandson. We may also note that Tewdrig, a Roman name, was used by the commanders/kings in Dumnonia and Gwent who may have been subordinate to Arthur II. It is interesting that Tewdrig's grandson was also called Athrwys.

Artur of Dalriada

Artur Mac Aedan was born in around 555AD and was the son of the King of Dalriada Aedan Mac Gabran. He was therefore a Scot. Artur never became a king. He was the son of Aedan, son of Gabran, son of Domangart, son of Fergus Mor. I have suggested that Arthwys ap Mar and Domangart Mac Fergus Mor could have been identical - and if this were the case that would make Artur the great grandson of Arthwys. All of the evidence that King Arthur fought in the North could equally be applied to Arthwys ap Mar - and of course he has the advantage of living at the right time and also being the right side of Hadrian's Wall. The name Morgan does crop up in Artur's family but despite his father being a renowned warrior, there is nothing to suggest he had a military career anything like that of Arthur and certainly would not have ruled the Britons, since he was a Scot.

Generation 7
The Arthur II Generation
C600-630

Note: Tewdrig of Gwent and Tewdrig of Dumnonia may be identical.

Generation 8 (Meurig and Noe's generation) C630-660

Noe: Dyfed
Meurig: Gwent
Iago: Gwynedd
Cynan: Powys
Medraut: Ergyng
Bili: Strathclyde
Domnall Brecc: Dal Riada

Saxons:

Eorcenbert: Kent
Sexred, Saeward, Saexbald, Sigefirth: Essex
Redwald: East Angles
Penda: Mercia
Edwin: Northumbria
Cuthwulf, Cynegils: Wessex

This generation is a significant one because it has both a son of an Arthur (Noe ap Arthur ap Pedr) and a Mordred (Medraut of Ergyng). It is of course possible that these two knew each other, and maybe fought each other, which could be intermingled with the memory of Arthwys and his brother Morydd.

Generation 8
The Meurig Generation
C630-660

Note: Noe was the son of Arthur II of Dyfed. Meurig was the father of Athrwys (Arthur III) of Gwent. Medraut (Mordred II) lived too late to be the Mordred of legend, who is Morydd in generation 4.

Generation 9: Athrwys ap Meurig's generation C650-700

Gwlyddien: Dyfed
Athrwys (Arthur III): Gwent
Cadfan & Cadwallon: Gwynedd
Selyf: Powys
Gwrfoddw: Ergyng
Owen: Strathclyde
Domangart II: Dal Riada

Saxons:

Egbert: Kent
Sebbi, Sigebert, Swithhelm, Sigibert II, Seleferth: Essex
Eorpwald: East Angles
Peada: Mercia
Eanfrith: Northumbria
Cenbert, Athelbald, Celowald: Wessex
Cuthred, Cenwealh, Centwine, Cyneburgh: Wessex

Athrwys ap Meurig

Athrwys ap Meurig was born in around 640AD. His father Meurig and grandfather Tewdrig were reasonably powerful kings in the Gwent area and it is possible that Tewdrig was also the Tewdrig that ruled Dumnonia after Peredur. If this is the case, Athrwys' great great great grandfather would have been Arthur's contemporary.

Conventional history suggests that Athrwys pre-deceased his father - but he made have served as a regent or ruled a client kingdom for him.

So why is Athrwys considered a contender for the historic King Arthur? How could a man born in the 7th century have fought the Saxons, succeeded Ambrosius and won Badon - a battle known to have been fought at least before the mid 6th century?

The most common and strongest arguments are:

1) He is called Athrwys, and sometimes Arthwys, which could easily be a variation of Arthur or Artorius.
2) He ruled the kingdom that included Caerleon, where Geoffrey says Arthur was crowned.
3) He ruled the kingdom that included the area where Arthur was said to have killed his son Anir.

So it is possible he was a King called Arthur by some, who reigned in the same place as "King Arthur." But unfortunately he did so at least 150 years too late. It is like suggesting that Churchill won the battle of Culloden. Yes he was a British leader, yes he won a great conflict, but the fact he was not born until 128 years after the battle, renders it impossible.

Other points of evidence for suggesting Athrwys was Arthur (Uther Pendragon was a title meaning "wonderful head of dragons" and could have been used by Tewdrig...) do not stand up to scrutiny. Athrwys has a well documented family tree and it does not resemble that of King Arthur in any way.

Although Athrwys or Antres is a very different name to Arthur, I will include him as Arthur III for the sake of easy identification. Even if Athrwys became king of Gwent (he probably did not – he died before his father Meurig) it is doubtful he was the most powerful of the British kings. That honour would go to Cadwallon of Gwynedd, but it seems likely that power had shifted to Penda and Peada of Mercia by this point.

Generation 9
The Athrwys (Arthur III) Generation
C660-700

Note: Athrwys may not have been a king in his own right

British overlords

Constantius (305-306)
Constantine I (306-337)
Constantine II (337-340)
Constans (337-350)
Octavius (350-383)[conjectural]
Magnus Maximus (383-388)
Eugenius (392-394)
Marcus (406)
Gratian (407)
Constantine III (407-411)
Agricola (411-430) *Coel Hen*
Vortigernus (430-466) *Ceneu*
Vitalis [usurper]
Vortimer (Morvawr, Mor, Uther) *Mar*
Ambrosius Aurelianus (466-485) *Pabo Post Prydain*
Artorius (485-540) *Arthwys ap Mar*
Eleutherius (540-560) *Elidyr*
Peredurus (560-580) *Pheredur*
Artorius II (580-620) *Arthur ap Pedr*

The riddle of Vortigern

The later Arthurian stories describe a power struggle between two dynasties. The House of Constantine is usurped by Vortigern and his son Vortimer, who make the foolish decision of inviting the Saxon Hengist to Britain as mercenaries.

Constantine's dynasty is restored by his sons Constans, Ambrosius and Uther, who is finally succeeded by his son Arthur. But some things do not add up about the story. Vortigern and Ambrosius are given such long life spans that many have concluded that there are two of each – Ambrosius the Elder, Vortigern Vitalis, Ambrosius Aurelianus and Vortigern Vortineu. Another aspect that does not add up about the story is that some sources give Vortigern three sons - Catigern, Pascent and

Faustus, but then Nennius gives him another son, called Vortimer, who seems to belong in the same generation as his father and also seems to have a completely opposing political view to his father. Vortigern is in bed with the Saxons (literally in one case) while Vortimer is, like Arthur, a defender against the Saxons. Vortigern and Vortimer battle to depose each other.

The natural conclusion would be that Vortimer was not a son of Vortigern, and was only assumed to be later because of their similar names. But Vortigern and Vortimer are both titles – compare to the later Vortipor.

Gildas in his De Excidio et Conquestu Britanniae (Source 1) tells how "all the councillors, together with that proud usurper" [omnes consiliarii una cum superbo tyranno] made the mistake of inviting "the fierce and impious Saxons" to settle in Britain. Note he does not name the Superbo Tyranno as Vortigern. Two later manuscripts name him as Uortigerno and Gurthigerno.

Gildas says a small group came at first and was settled "on the eastern side of the island, by the invitation of the unlucky [infaustus] usurper". This could of course be Northumbria, as easily as, say, Kent.

Gildas does not mention Vortipor. This does not enter the story until Nennius. In Nennius, Vortimer "(fought) valiantly against Hengist, Horsa, and his people," and, after Horsa's death, he fought against Octha, who then came down from the north to rule with his father. Vortimer fought against 'them' at Thanet. A list of four battles follows, which are often assumed to be around Kent, but as we will see later, are not necessarily so.

So why does Vortimer have equal claim to the throne as his father whose views he opposes? How is Vortimer a defender of the realm like Arthur? But not mentioned as such by other sources?

The true origin of Vortigern seems to not be found in the south but in the north with the historic rulers Coel, his son Ceneu and his son-in-law Cunedda. We will return to the origin of Vortimer.

Coel was recorded as 'Coel Hen Gautepauc' which translates as Coel Hen Vortipor, and Ceneu's name is seen as Vortigern Vortineu.

Genealogies would seem to suggest two men. In some records we see a "Vortigern the thin" – seemingly to distinguish himself from another Vortigern. We also see two wives - we have Vortigern marrying Severa, the daughter of Maximus, in about 425 (Vortigern would therefore have been born about 400). In about 455 we then have a Vortigern marrying Rowena, daughter of the Saxon Hengist. Vortigern is credited with sons named Catigern, Paschent and Vortimer, which parallels the later Dyfed chronology where Vortipor is succeeded by Congair and Pets.

If Vortigern Vorteneu, who married the daughter of Maximus, had a flourit of the mid 5th century, he corresponds perfectly with Ceneu ap Coel and Vorteneu with Ceneu.

The Coel-Vortigern lineage

The "Life of St. Beuno" gives the following lineage:
Belim (Beli Mawr)
Amalech
Auallach
Eudoleu
Eudos
Elud
Eudegern
Eudegan
Deheuwynt
Rittegyrn
Gorthegyrnn (Vortigern)
Gortheyrnn (Vortimer)

Compare this to the lineage of Coel Hen, given in the Harleian:
Beli
Aballac
Eudelen

Eudos
Ebiud
Outigern
Oudecant
Ritigirn
Iumetel
Grat
Urban
Telpuil
Teuhant
Tecmant
Coyl Hen Guotepauc

Not only is Coel given the epithet Guotepauc (Vortipor), his ancestors also have the 'Tigern' name and the common ancestry through Ritigern. If we return to our map, it is clear that the Vortigern dynasty began with Coel and his son Ceneu.

In Pennine Dragon, I identified 'Ambrosius the Younger' with Pabo Post Prydain, and in this case the 'Vortigern the Thin' who they had a rivalry with, was an unrelated king. The other usurping Vortigern was Vitalis, the Vortigern who married Severa, daughter of Magnus Maximus. He would have been born in around 400AD. This Vortigern was also known as Vortigern the Very Thin (Gwrtheyrn Gwrtheneu), said to be the son of Gwidol, but we will return to him later.

Vortimer, the valiant king who battled against the Saxons was Mar (Mor) son of Ceneu. Not only was Mar the real Uther Pendragon, he was also the real Vortimer.

Vortimer and Mar

In the Cornish chronology he was called Mor-vawr (Mor Uther) here he is called Vorti-Mor. If Vortimer (Gwerthefyr) and Mor (Uthyr) were identical, this brings a fascinating new Arthurian dimension – since Vortimer was the father of Madrun and Anna, which is an obvious contrast with Uther, father of Morgan and Anna.

We again have a new chronology, which, rather than making things more complicated, actually simplifies matters:

Protectors of Britain after Rome

1) Coel Hen Vortepauc: Protector of Britain (Agricola)
2) Ceneu ap Coel Vortepauc (Vortigern Vorteneu)
- Vortigern Vitalis - usurper
3) Morvawr (Vortimer, Uther Pendragon, Mar)
4) Arthur (Arthwys)
5) Kynvelin, Keidyaw and Eleuther (sons of Arthur)
6) Peredur
7) Arthur II

Vortimer's battles

At this point we have identified Vortigern with Ceneu ap Coel Hen Vortepauc, and Vortimer with his son Mar. Now earlier on we established that Mar was Iubher/Ebrauc/Uther – the king of York. So how can this king of York, who fathered Arthwys of Ebrauc, also be Vortimer whose battles took place in London and Kent? The answer is because Vortimer's battles were not in London at all - they were in the Yorkshire area.

The Historia tells us:

et guorthemir contra illos quattuor bella auide gessit. primum bellum super flumen derguentid; secundum bellum super uadum, quod dicitur in lingua eorum episford, in nostra autem lingua rithergabail, et ibi cecidit hors cum filio guorthigirni, cuius nomen erat categirn. tertium bellum in campo iuxta lapidem tituli, qui est super ripam gallici maris, commisit et barbari uicti sunt et ille uictor fuit et ipsi in fugam uersi usque ad ciulas suas mersi sunt in eas muliebriter intrantes.

Four times did Vortimer valorously encounter the enemy; the first has been mentioned, the second was upon the river Darent, the third at the Ford, in their language called Epsford, though in ours Set thirgabail, there Horsa fell, and Catigern, the son of Vortigern; the fourth battle he fought, was near the stone on the shore of the Gallic sea, where the Saxons being defeated, fled to their ships.

While Nennius is translating the place name as Epsford, the older Anglo Saxon Chronicle uses Aegaelesprep which could easily have evolved into Adlethorpe in Skegness.

Nennius' Darent could of course be the River Derwent north of Doncaster, and the Anglo Saxon Chronicle's account of them then moving to Lundenbyrg and Centlond (of course normally translated as London and Kent) could easily be Londesborough near Beverley and Cantley near Doncaster. Crecganford could be Glanford Bridge (Brigg).

In other words - all of Vortimer's battles can be located just east of York.

By understanding that:

Mar = Mor = Vortimor = Morvawr = Mor Uthyr = Uther

We can understand that Uther and Vortimer were both names for the same man, the king of York and the father of Arthur.

Vortigern Vitalis – the other Vortigern

Coel obviously lived to an old age (Hen means old), his life could have spanned anything from about 380 to 470. Coel could have held rank during the Roman occupation - perhaps as Dux Bellorum and then saw himself as 'protector' after Rome withdrew.

During his reign, Niall of the Nine Hostages made excursions to Britain, something continued by his descendants. His son Laogaire may have been the origin for Guinevere's legendary father Leodegraunce. Coel passed the mantle of Protector to his son Ceneu and it is Ceneu that accounts for the Vortigern Vortineu of legend. Ceneu was succeeded in this position by his son Mar who became Vorti-Mar. However, some of the tales of Vortigern, as we find them in Nennius, were derived from Irish sources.

I have studied the 'Annals of the Four Masters' for many years as they record the exploits of my own family. My paternal clan, Keegan (MacAodhagain) is recorded in dozens of entries in the work, since they were hereditary Brehons and Ollamhs. And in this book we find the source of Nennius' Vortigern - the one who encountered dragons. In Ireland he was known as Foirtchernn.

The Annals of the Kingdom of Ireland, or The Annals of the Four Masters as they are more commonly called, were compiled between 1632 and 1636 under the direction of Michael O'Clery, a Franciscan brother in Donegal. They are a yearly chronicles of major (and sometimes minor) occurrances in Ireland from the Year of the Deluge (ie Noah's flood) until 1616 A.D.

They tell how the Irish high king Laogaire had a grandson named Foirtchernn born around 440 in County Meath and he had a British mother called Scotnoe. He is recorded in the Martyrology of Tallaght:

Lomman i nAth Truim cum suis omnibus et Fortchern.

The Martyrology of Oengus also mentions him calling him Fortchern the Scaley.

The Martyrology of Donegal records the associations of him with St Patrick and the royal background of Forthchern:

Foirtchern, son of Feidhlimidh, son of Laoghaire, son of Niall of the Nine Hostages. He was a bishop, and a disciple of Patrick, and he was of Ath-Truim in Laoghaire, and of Cill Foirtcheirn in Ui-Dróna, in Leinster.

So - what does the hagiography of Saint Patrick record of our saints? Below is an account taken from the diocesan historian of County Meath, Father Anthony Cogan, which includes an extract from the writings of Tirechan: And then we find what is possibly the origin of Nennius' story.

In the Life of St Columba the Saint visited (the unidentified but probably Irish) Mount Cainle and had to rule in a case against some magicians, and was entertained by the 'rich plebeius' named Foirtgirn. The ecclesiastical origin of Trim is accounted for by Tirechan, a writer of the seventh century records:

"A.D. 433. When Patrick, in his holy navigation, came to Ireland, he left St. Loman at the mouth of the Boyne to take care of his boat forty days and forty nights; and then he (St. Loman) waited another forty, out of obedience to Patrick. Then, according to the order of his master (the Lord being his pilot), he came in his boat, against the stream, as far as the ford of Trim, near the fort of Feidilmid, son of Loiguire.

"And when it was morning, Foirtchern, son of Feidilmid, found him reciting the Gospel, and admiring the Gospel and his doctrine, immediately believed; and a well being opened in that place, he was baptized by Loman in Christ, and remained with him until his mother came to look for him; and she was made glad at his sight, because she was a British woman. But she likewise believed, and again returned to her house, and told to her husband all that had happened to her and her son.

"And then Feidilmid was glad at the coming of the priest, because he had his mother from the Britons, the daughter of the king of the Britons, namely, Scothnoessa. And Feidilmid saluted Loman in the British tongue, asking him, in order, of his faith and kindred, and he answered: 'I am Loman, a Briton, a Christian, a disciple of Bishop Patrick, who is sent from the Lord to baptize the people of the Irish, and to convert them to the faith of Christ, who sent me here according to the will of God'.

"And immediately Feidilmid believed, with all his family, and dedicated (immolavit) to him and St. Patrick his country, with his possessions and with all his family; all these he dedicated to

Patrick and Loman, with his son Fortchern, till the Day of Judgment. But Feidilmid crossed the Boyne, and Loman remained with Fortchern in Trim, until Patrick came to them, and built a church with them, twenty-two years before the foundation of the Church of Armagh".

In the Annals of the Four Masters, at 432, we read:

"Ath-Truim was founded by Patrick, it having been granted by Fedhlim, son of Laoghaire, son of Niall, to God and to him, Loman and Fortchern".

The Irish Fortchern was the usurper, Ceneu was Vortigern Vortineu and Mar was Vortimer. Now we can understand how and why these characters are so misunderstood.

Arthur and Cerdic

Part of the riddle of Arthur is - how could the man have been so successful, when his reign coincided with that of the Saxon patriarch, Cerdic? How could Cerdic be conquering land left, right and centre when Arthur was supposedly leaving Britain in 20 years of peace after Badon? The answer is simply they were on the same side! The Romans employed Celtic and Germanic troops alike, and by the 6th and 7th century a British king was every bit as likely to form an alliance with a Saxon king as he was a British one.

But Cerdic was not a Saxon King. He was a British prince, and he was the brother of Arthur. Arthur was Dux Bellorum, Cerdic was Dux Gewissae.

This is another detail hidden in plain sight. Both in the Arthurian legends and in the generalogies. In the Arthurian legends, Cerdic is remembered as Caradoc Vreichvras, and later as Sir Carados. I do not claim he and Arthur never had a cross word! But for much of their flourit they were allies.

According to the Saxon genealogies, Cerdic was the son of Elessa, father of Creoda and grandfather of Cynric.

According to the British genealogies (Hafod MS. 19 1536) Caradoc was the son of Llyr, father of Kowrda and grandfather of Kydeboc.

Creoda and Cynric are obviously similar to Kowrda and Kydeboc, but let us take it further still. In the Bonedd, Kowrda is the ancestor of Kathan, the same as Cerdic's descendant Cutha.

So where does Elessa and Llyr come into it? In some legends of Caradoc, the name of Llyr merini, is given as Eliavres – very similar to Cerdic's father Elessa. And while Creoda is given Cynric as a son, Caradoc has Meuric.

The final piece to the puzzle is that Arthwys ap Mar has a brother called Ceretic, and this is the British name for Cerdic. Llyr Marini (Llyr of the Sea) is the same as Mor (sea). 'Lehr marini' would be `master of the sea', `teacher of the sea', or perhaps `wizard of the sea'.

There is no way Arthur and Cerdic could co-exist unless they were allies. The theory of Arthur and Cerdic being allies makes perfect sense. Let's look at the evidence:

Arthur's 12 battles named by Nennius took place in around 490-520. Most of these battles are clearly placed around Northumbria and between Hadrian's and Antonian Walls. For example Celidon, Agned (Edinburgh) and Glein (Northumbria) and then there were the battles fought in Chester (City of the Legions), Durham (Guinnion Fort) and Wigan (Dubglas).

After Badon there was a generation of peace. This can be expressed as between 516, when Arthur won at Badon, and 547 when Ida took Bernicia. At the very same time that Arthur was defeating the Angles, Cerdic was ruling in the south. He was winning battles in Hampshire and Portsmouth and ruling all the way up until 534. So how could Arthur's reign have been one of victory if all the time Cerdic was winning? They were on the same side. Because they were brothers, sons of Mar.

Like their ancestors Coel Hen and Efdaf Hen respectively, Arthur and Cerdic were the Dux Bellorum and Dux Gewissae.

Arthur was responsible for defending the north. Cerdic was responsible for defending the south coast.

Cerdic of Wessex is called in early sources "dux gewissorum", that is, "duke of the Gewissae". The British client-king, Octavius, who appears in ancient Welsh annals as Eudaf "Hen", who reigned in Britain during the Roman Era, was called "dux gewissorum" as an officer in Roman service before his usurpation of the British throne. And, the Dark Age "proud tyrant" Vortigern is referred to as "dux gewissorum" before he became King of Britain. Bede says that the West Saxons, who gave Wessex its name, were originally called "Gewissae" too.

Another clue to Cerdic's nationality is given by St. Gildas, who was a contemporary of Cerdic. He wrote in his "De Excidio" that the British victory at the Battle of Badon Hill [or Mount Badon], was so decisive that it gave the Britons a generation free from "barbarian" ["Saxon"] attacks, though the peace was often broken by the Britons fighting in civil wars among themselves.

The glaring contradiction between St. Gildas' assertion in his "De Excidio" that Britain was free of "barbarian" attacks for a generation - maybe St. Gildas did not consider Cerdic to have been a Saxon, but a Briton; nor the Wessex kingdom to have been a barbarian ["Saxon"] kingdom.

Arthwys and Cerdic were co-rulers of Britain - one was the Dux Bellorum, the other Dux Gewissorum. One made his base in York, the other in Wessex.

Lineage of Mordred I
Mar (Mor)
Morydd (Mordred I)
Madog
Myrddin (Merlin)

Lineage of Mordred II
Mar (Mor, Llyr Marini)
Cerdic (Caradoc)
Creoda (Cawrdaf)
Medraut (Mordred II)

Lineage of Cerdic
Mar (Mor)
Cynric (Kydebog)
Ceawlin (Kollen) and Cutha

Lineage of Arthur
Mar (Mor)
Arthwys (Arthur Penuchel)
Keidyaw
Gwendollau (Myrddin's master)

The Anglo Saxon Chronicles

Before we look at the British sources, let's look at Cerdic's battles in the Saxon chronicles.

495AD: This year came two leaders into Britain, Cerdic and Cynric his son, with five ships, at a place that is called Cerdic's-ore. And they fought with the Welsh the same day. [When he eventually] died, his son Cynric succeeded to the government, and held it six and twenty winters. Then he died; and Ceawlin, his son, succeeded, who reigned seventeen years. Then he died; and Ceol succeeded to the government, and reigned five years. When he died, Ceolwulf, his brother, succeeded, and reigned seventeen years...

508AD: This year Cerdic and Cynric slew a British king, whose name was Natanleod, and five thousand men with him. After this was the land named Netley, from him, as far as Charford.

Note: Cerdic is already referred to in Britain in 495 and 508, it is not until 514 that it says the West Saxons came:

514AD: This year came the West-Saxons into Britain, with three ships, at the place that is called Cerdic's-ore. And Stuff and Wihtgar fought with the Britons, and put them to flight.

Note: This period would co-incide with Arthur's northern battles.

Here the chronicles say Cerdic only undertook the government of the Saxons in 519AD – after Badon.

519AD: This year Cerdic and Cynric undertook the government of the West-Saxons; the same year they fought with the Britons at a place now called Charford. From that day have reigned the children of the West-Saxon kings.

527AD: This year Cerdic and Cynric fought with the Britons in the place that is called Cerdic's-ley.

530AD: This year Cerdic and Cynric took the isle of Wight, and slew many men in Carisbrook.

534AD: This year died Cerdic, the first king of the West-Saxons. Cynric his son succeeded to the government, and reigned afterwards twenty-six winters. And they gave to their two nephews, Stuff and Wihtgar, the whole of the Isle of Wight.

Note: According to the Annales Cambrae, Arthur died in 537-539 and the Angle Saxon Chronicle says the sun was eclipsed after this. A coincidence obviously but one that could have added to Arthur's legend.

538AD: This year the sun was eclipsed, fourteen days before the calends of March, from before morning until nine.

Note: It is here that Nennius places Arthur's reign also.

547AD: This year Ida began his reign; from whom first arose the royal kindred of the Northumbrians…

PART THREE

THE LOST BOOKS OF ARTHUR

The Books of Arthur

I, Nennius, disciple of St. Elbotus, have endeavoured to write some extracts which the dulness of the British nation had cast away, because teachers had no knowledge, nor gave any information in their books about this island of Britain. But I have got together all that I could find as well from the annals of the Romans as from the chronicles of the sacred fathers, Hieronymus, Eusebius, Isidorus, Prosper, and from the annals of the Scots and Saxons, and from our ancient traditions. Many teachers and scribes have attempted to write this, but somehow or other have abandoned it from its difficulty, wither on account of frequent deaths, or the often recurring calamities of war. I pray that every reader who shall read this book, may pardon me, for having attempted, like a chattering jay, or like some weak witness, to write these things, after they had failed. I yield to him who knows more of these things than I do.

Nennius, Historia Brittonum

Source 1: Gildas

Gildas' is not one of the lost books, but he is a primary source. Gildas lived at around the time of Arthur, although he was probably a little younger. Later stories have Arthur feuding with Gildas' brother Huell to explain why Gildas doesn't mention Arthur. However a simpler explanation is:

1)   Gildas barely names anyone
2)   Almost everyone he does name, he likens to an animal.
Therefore when he mentions The Bear he is referring to Arthur.

Gildas:
"You bear, you rider and ruler of many, and guider of the chariot which is the receptacle of the bear"

The Latin phrase "et tu ab adolescentiae annis urse multorum sessor, aurigaque currus receptaculi urse" when translated into Welsh becomes: A ydych yn dwyn llawer yn reidiwr o'r blynyddoedd cynnar , car aurigaque **arth** cynhwysydd.

Gildas wrote in living memory of Arthur, perhaps about 10 years after Arthur's death. Although he mentioned Arth in the paragraph addressing Cuneglas (son of Owain son of Einion son of Cunedda), Cuneglas was one of the Votadini (otherwise known as the Gododdin).

Gildas says of Ambrosius:

That they might not be brought to utter destruction, took arms under the conduct of Ambrosius Aurelianus, a modest man, who of all the Roman nation was then alone in the confusion of this troubled period by chance left alive. His parents, who for their merit were adorned with the purple, had been slain in these same broils, and now his progeny in these our days, although shamefully degenerated from the worthiness of their ancestors, provoke to battle their cruel conquerors, and by the goodness of our Lord obtain the victory. After this, sometimes our countrymen, sometimes the enemy, won the field, to the end that our Lord might this land try after his accustomed manner these his Israelites, whether they loved him or not, until the year of the siege of the Badonic hill, when took place also the last almost, though not the least slaughter of our cruel foes, which was a fact I know forty-four years and it also the time of my own nativity. And yet neither to this day are the cities of our country inhabited as before, but being forsaken and overthrown, still lie desolate; our foreign wars having ceased, but our civil troubles still remaining. For as well the remembrance of such a terrible desolation of the island, as also of the unexpected recovery of the same, remained in the minds of those who were eyewitnesses of the wonderful events of both, and in regard thereof, kings, public magistrates, and private persons, with priests and clergymen, did all and every one of them live orderly according to their several vocations.

SOURCE 2: Anieirin

Anierin is a great source for Arthur, because it firmly places him as a British warleader fighting the Angles.

Anierin:
He brought black crows to a fort's wall, though he was not Arthur. He made his strength a refuge, the front line's bulwark, Gwawrddur.

Anierin or Neirin's Gododdin tells of a great Romano-British warrior called Gwawrddur who, although valiant, was "not Arthur." This comparison suggests that Arthur was likewise and when we consider the northern location of the Gododdin – Catterick in North Yorkshire, it seems more than likely his subject was Arthur Penuchel, who ruled that area a generation earlier.

We should note, Anierin also provides us with the first mention of Merlin (Myrddin) who he calls Mirdyn. One manuscript has the lines:

amuc moryen gwenwawt mirdyn. a chyvrannv penn prif eg weryt...

Morien defended the fair song of Myrddin and laid the head of a chief in the earth...

It seems that Anierin is largely an independent source. It doesn't seem to have influenced the later Arthurian sources, neither does he seem to have been influenced by Gildas. Anierin was a bard who served kings of Rheged, Gildas was a monk with an axe to grind.

Prince Aneirin of Flowing Verse was a younger son of King Dunaut Bwr (the Stout) of the Northern Pennines, is one of the best known of ancient Celtic bards. He was sometimes known as Aneirin Awenyd - the Inspired - and was described by his near contemporaries as High-King of Bards or Prince of Poets.

He was apparently present at the Battle of Catraeth, between a British coalition under King Mynyddog Mwynfawr (the Wealthy) of Din-Eityn and the Anglians of Northumbria. Here he wrote the now famous poem, Y Gododdin. Though the surviving text has become corrupted and added to, the core section is believed to have actually been written by this man around the year 600, in living memory of Arthur.

The poetry tells us that Aneirin was present at this battle and, having been taken prisoner, was one of only four (or two) Brythonic survivors. He remained a captive until his ransom was paid by Ceneu ap Llywarch Hen, another northern British bard who made reference to Arthur.

The Book of Aneirin begins with the introduction Hwn yw e gododin. aneirin ae cant ("This is the Gododdin; Aneirin sang it"). The first stanza appears to be a reciter's prologue, composed after the death of Aneirin:

Gododin, gomynaf oth blegyt yg gwyd cant en aryal en emwyt:
Er pan want maws mur trin,er pan aeth daear ar Aneirin,
nu neut ysgaras nat a Gododin.

Gododdin, I make claim on thy behalf In the presence of the throng boldly in the court: Since the gentle one, the wall of battle, was slain, Since earth covered Aneirin, Poetry is now parted from the Gododdin.

.

SOURCE 3: Taliesin

Taliesin is a fascinating source because he may have actually known Arthur and written about him in records we still have. Therefore he is potentially the most primary of sources.

Unfortunately we do not have original manuscripts and his work may have been heavily edited over the years. Although most of Taliesin's work is in praise of Urien Rheged, he does mention Arthur, Gwallawg and Uther.

Taliesin says of Arthur:

Did not (he) lead from Cawrnur
Horses pale supporting burdens?
The sovereign elder.
The generous feeder.
The third deep wise one,
To bless Arthur,
Arthur the blessed,
In a compact song.
On the face in battle

From the loricated Legion,
Arose the Guledig,
Around the old renowned boundary.

Although the manuscript that contains this poem is a later copy, it is interesting because Taliesin, like Anierin and Rhun, was a Northern bard who lived within a generation or two of Arthur and his "loricated Legion" and "old renowned boundary" conjure up images of nowhere other than the Roman garrisons of Hadrian's Wall.

Gildas, Anierin and Taliesin lived in living memory of Arthur Penuchel, a hero of the Gododdin, a mighty Bear who ruled as Guletic with his Legion, from Hadrian's Wall across what is now Yorkshire. A man whose grandsons fought the battle of Arthuret.

Taliesin says of Uther:

Am I not with hosts making a din?
I would not cease, between two hosts, without gore.
Am I not he that is called Gorlassar?

My belt was a rainbow to my foe.
Am I not a prince, in darkness,
(To him) that takes my appearance with my two chief baskets?
Am I not, like Cawyl, ploughing?
I would not cease without gore between two hosts.
Is it not I that will defend my sanctuary?
In separating with the friends of wrath.
Have I not been accustomed to blood about the wrathful,
A sword-stroke daring against the sons of Cawrnur?
I shared my shelter,
a ninth share in Arthur's valour.
I broke a hundred forts.
I slew a hundred stewards.
I bestowed a hundred mantles.
I cut off a hundred heads.
I gave to an old chief
very great swords of protection.
Is it not I that performed the rights of purification,
When Hayarndor went to the top of the mountain?
To my deprivation, to my sorrow, sinew was brave.
The world would not be if not for my offspring.
I am a bard to be praised. The unskilful
May he be possessed by the ravens and eagle and bird of wrath.
Avagddu came to him with his equal,
When the bands of four men feed between two plains.
Abiding in heaven was he, my desire,
Against the eagle, against the fear of the unskilful.
I am a bard, and I am a harper,
I am a piper, and I am a crowder.
Of seven score musicians the very great enchanter.
There was of the enamelled honor the privilege.
Hu of the expanded wings.
Thy son, thy barded proclamation,
Thy steward, of a gifted father.
My tongue to recite my death-song.
If of stone-work the opposing wall of the world.
May the countenance of Prydain be bright for my guidance.

Sovereign of heaven, let my messages not be rejected

Here, two things are significant - firstly he takes 'a share of Arthur's valour, and secondly says he was *called Gorlassar –* could this be the origin of Uther shapeshifting into Gorlois?

The Spoils of Annwn found in the Book of Taliesin makes another account of Arthur. If the later Culhwch owes some of its narrative to Pa Gur (Arthur's gatekeeper, Kei and Bedwyr), it is from Annwn that Culhwch borrows the tale of Arthur sailing to the Otherworld (or probably Ireland). We later realise that the origin of the tales is Arthwys and his brother Llaenauc meeting Cywair in Ireland.

I praise the Lord, Prince of the realm and King!
His rule extends across the whole wide world.
Gweir was penned beneath the fortress mound,
As tell the tales of Pwyll and Pryderi.
None before him passed into the prison,
With a heavy chain a faithful servant bound.
Bitter before the spoils of Annwn he sang,
And until Doomsday lasts our bardic prayer.
Three companies of warriors we went in –
Seven alone rose up from Elfs-castle.

Song rang out, honoring me with praise
In the four-peaked fortress, four its mighty turnings.
My verses from within the cauldron uttered,
By breath of maidens ninefold they were kindled.
The lord of Annwn's cauldron: how is it made?
A dark ridge on its border, crusted pearls.
Its fate is not to boil the meat of cowards,
The deadly flashing sword is lifted to it,
And in the hand of the Leaper it was left.
Before the doors of hell the lamps were burning.
When we went in with Arthur, blinding trouble –
Seven alone rose up from Meads-castle.

Song rang out, honoring me with praise
In the four-peaked fortress, isle of the strong door.
Flowing water and shining jet are mingled,
They drink the sparkling wine before their followers.
Three companies of warriors sailed the sea –
Seven alone rose up from Hard-castle.

I do not deserve to be put with poetasters:
Beyond the fort they missed the valor of Arthur.
Six thousand men stood on the glass wall,
Their sentinel was difficult to speak with.
Three companies of warriors went with Arthur –
Seven alone rose up from Guts-castle.

I do not deserve the mean men, slack their shield straps.
They do not know the day of our creation,
Nor what time of day the One was born.
Who made him who strayed far from Defwy meadows?
They do not know the ox, his thick headband,
Full sevenscore links upon his chained collar.
And when we went with Arthur, woeful visit –
Seven alone rose up from Gods-castle.

I do not deserve these men -- slack their will.
They do not know which day the chief was sired,
Nor what hour of day the lord was born,
Nor what beasts are kept, their heads of silver.
When we went in with Arthur, sorrowful strife –
Seven alone rose up from Box-castle.

Monks are a pack together -- a choir of dogs –
They shrink away from meeting the lords who know:
Is there one course of wind? One course of water?
Is there one spark of fire? Of fierce tumult?

Monks are a pack together, like youngling wolves
They shrink away from meeting the lords who know:

They do not know when night and dawn divide,
Nor wind, what is its course, nor what its onrush,
What place it ravages, nor where it strikes.
The grave of the saint vanishes, grave and ground.
I praise the Lord, great Prince of the whole world,
And so I am not sad, for Christ endows me.

One thing is clear – Uther was not from the imagination of Geoffrey of Monmouth. In Pa Gur one of Arthur's companions is given as "Mabon ap Mydron, servant of Uthir Pen Dragon". The Book of Taliesin mentions Arthur and is named after Uther himself as **Marvnat Uthyr Pen**.

The unusual Welsh poem Ymiddiddan Arthur a'r Eryr ("The Dialogue of Arthur and the Eagle") identifies the eagle as Eliwlat mab Madawc mab Uthyr and a nephew of Arthur. Thereby suggesting Uther was also Arthur's father.

yng|kor y keuri gerllaw emreis y vrawt y kladpwyt vthyr benn dragon yn vernhinyawl ESTORIA **ARTHVR UA⊁ B UTHYR** YW HONO OLL OLL GWEDY **MARW VTHYRR BENN DRAGON**

Now we can understand how the man nicknamed 'Iubher' (Ebrauc/York) in the Gaelic language became Uther to the Welsh, and Mar in the king lists.

SOURCE 4: The Lost Book of Arthur
Written by Rhun ap Urien

There can be little contention that the record I refer to as The Lost Book of Arthur existed. This is the source that names Arthur's battles, the source used by Nennius and as I established earlier, the Chartres manuscript actually identifies the son of Urien as its author.

We know that Badon was a historic event from Gildas (Source 1), and we know that Arthur fought in battle such as this from Anierin (Source 2) and we know that Arthur was Guletic along Hadrian's Wall from Taliesin (Source 3) and now we come to Source 4, the source from which Nennius was working when he listed Arthur's 12 battles.

By identifying Arthur with Arthwys ap Mar, we can understand where these battles would have taken place and by referring to the other sources we can see that Hadrian's Wall is a good place to start looking.

In constructing the narrative of the Lost Book of Arthur, I will assume that Nennius has recorded the information as faithfully as possible. Nennius used Source 1 to construct his narrative on Vortigern and Ambrosius and then he used Source 4 to construct his narrative on Arthur. But when we look at all the evidence, we see something that was hidden in plain sight. Nennius was only the later editor of this work. He actually names the man who contributed the bulk of the sections. And he named that man Filius Urbgen – the son of Urien.

What we must understand is that the Historia we know today can be found in various surviving manuscripts – and they all differ slightly. Sadly the oldest manuscript – known as the Chartres Manuscript or the Chartres Rescension was destroyed by a World War 2 blitz. In this manuscript Nennius is not named as the author at all – the son of Urien is. Therefore, despite the sizeable contribution by Gildas, the parts about the Northern British and Angle kings like Arthur and Ida were written by Rhun.

To put it into context, Arthur was a contemporary and cousin of Meirchionn (the king Mark of the romances). Arthur was succeeded by his sons Keidyaw and Eleuther, and Meirchionn by Urien. As Keidyaw's son and Eleuther's sons squabbled over the kingdom, Urien was succeeded by his son Owain, Eleuther by his son Peredur and Arthur's brother Llaenauc by his son Gwallawg. Owain, Peredur and Gwallawg (Sir Galahad, Sir Perceval and Sir Owen) formed a coalition. Owain's brother was Rhun, who was a monk and scribe rather than a warrior king.

Rhun is actually mentioned in the Historia three times:

- Rhun is cited in the oldest manuscript as the author
- Rhun is claimed to be the bishop who baptized Edwin of Deira. "Edwin, son of Alla, reigned seventeen years, seized on Elmete, and expelled Cerdic, its king.... The following Easter Edwin himself received baptism, and twelve thousand of his subjects with him. If any one wishes to know who baptized them, it was Rum Map Urbgen."
- Oswiu of Northumbria's first wife is listed as Rheinmellt, daughter of Royth, son of Rhun.

Now we can start to understand the **Lost Book of Arthur.** As the greatest king of the north, he was remembered by northern bards like Taliesin and Aneirin but also now by Rhun of Rheged whose father Urien, brother Owain and grandfather Meirchionn actually fought alongside Arthur, his son Eleuther and his grandson Peredur.

Mythical King Arthur and his kin

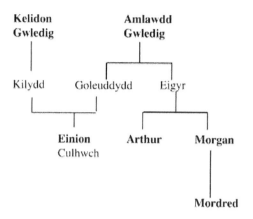

Historic King Arthwys and his kin

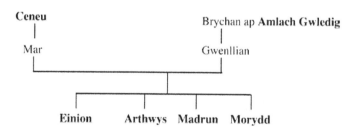

Arthur's first battle: The River Glein

Arthur, like his father Mar, grandfather Ceneu and great grandfather Coel, held a very significant position on Hadrian's Wall. This was the northern pinnacle of the Roman Empire and the last line of defence against the Scots and Picts. As the great Bull Protector of the Sixth Legion, Arthur governed on forts like Banna and his brother Morydd on Camboglanna.

The first battle Arthur is recorded as having won was nearby. Rhun recorded:

Then Arthur fought against them in those days, together with the kings of the British; but he was their Dux Bellorum. The first battle was at the mouth of the river called Glein.

The River Glen is a seven mile long tributary of the River Till, flowing through Northumberland. The College Burn and Bowmont Water meet near Kirknewton to form the River Glen.

The Glen flows past the small settlements of Yeavering, Lanton, Coupland, Akeld and Ewart, before joining the Till. The area around the Glen is rich in historical and archaeological interest. Iron Age hilltop forts on peaks to the south of the river overlook the Anglian settlement and palace site at Yeavering, where in 627AD St. Paulinus baptised new converts over 36 days and, according to Bede, "washed them with the water of absolution in the river Glen, which is close by."

The area around the Glen was the setting for some of the bloodiest border warfare between Scotland and England. The Battle of Humbleton Hill was fought near the river in 1402, as was the Battle of Geteryne (Yeavering) in 1415.

In a field to the north of Yeavering Bell, to the south of the road as you pass the hill, is the Yeavering Battle Stone. This Bronze Age megalith stands in an area where remains of burial pits and the debris of Mesolithic flint working have been found.

In 1415 it took on new meaning and significance when it became seen as marking the spot where Sir Robert Umfraville and the Earl of Westmorland, with 140 spearmen and 300 bowmen, defeated 4000 Scots. However the stone was already very ancient when King Edwin dined at Ad Gefrin, several centuries before the battle the stone is thought to commemorate took place. The stone is associated with a henge.

The Yeavering Bell hill-fort, prior to becoming a Saxon stronghold, was the British Gefrin. Gefrin, according to Eilert Ekwall (in The Concise Oxford Dictionary of English Place-Names), is from the Welsh word gafr 'goat' or a compound containing gafr plus Welsh bryn, for "Goat-hill". Interestingly Otranto Cathedral in Italy shows a mosaic of Arthur dating back to the 1160s riding a goat on a quest, as featured on the cover design of this book. Along with Modena Cathedral, they are some of the oldest depictions of Arthur. In fact the picture of Arthur on the cover of this book may well be the oldest picture (aside from carvings) that survives of Arthur.

Could this battle have led to a legend of Arthur at Goat Hill? And subsequently we get the images of Arthur riding a goat.

There was also a Gaulish god conflated with Mercury called Gebrinius. It is possible that Gefrin represents a British counterpart of this divine name.

Excavations revealed a complex of great halls or palaces, some over eighty five feet (26m) in length, of timber construction and built to a very high standard. Ancillary buildings were found, such as kitchens, a weaving shed, and what the excavator believed to have been a pagan temple converted to Christian use.

The palace complex was designed to accomodate elements of the earlier landscape - notably two burial monuments and the massive 'Great Enclosure'. This Great Enclosure's prime function is thought to have been as a kraal for cattle brought to the site perhaps as taxation or to be consumed during feasts.

The Gefrin Trust (see gefrin.com) writes: "Building work began in the 6th century, the foundations of the timber halls cutting through the remains of religious monuments and the cemetery of Neolithic and Early Bronze Age people living here some 3000 years earlier."

Therefore we see from Bede it was a significant location at the time. We see from archaeology there were Iron Age forts, and we see from subsequent battles it was a strategic location. We have found Arthur's first battle site.

The 'battle stone' seems to confirm that a notable battle of yore was fought there and it is nearby to Arthur's base at Hadrian's Wall and his Gododdin kingdom.

The Glen in Northumbria as Arthur's first battle:

• There are only two rivers called Glen. The other is in Lincolnshire. The one in Northumbria is of strategic importance.
• It is in the Kingdom of Arthwys
• It is near to Din Gyardi (Dolorous Garde) where Arthwys' brother Llaenauc (later Lleminawc and Lancelot) ruled
• There was a fortress in the 6th century
• It is mentioned by Bede and was used for Christian baptisms

- Archaeology shows it was inhabited by Britons and Saxons
- There was a battle there – marked by a battle stone
- It relates to the legend of Arthur and the Goat

Is the River Glen in Northumbria the most likely candidate for the River Glein? In light of this information it is the only serious candidate for the River Glein.

Northumbria is accepted to be one of the most likely candidates for Arthur's first battle and not only have we identified Arthurian folklore nearby, we have also discovered precise battle sites. The site of Glein is one of the strongest pieces of evidence that the historic King Arthur was a man of the North.

Arthur's second, third, fourth and fifth battles: The River Dubglas

Rhun tells us:

The second, third, fourth, and fifth, were on another river, by the Britons called Duglas, in the region Linuis.

In presenting the hypothesis for Arthwys as Arthur, the most likely site for the battle of Dubglas is the Douglas in Wigan. Towards the end of this book we will look at an alternative based on the suggestion that Arthur II may have been responsible for some of Arthur's legacy, but for now we will concentrate on the evidence that Arthur's battles were fought by Arthur I in the traditional time frame.

The identification of Douglas as Dubglas is not purely based on the name. Again we have to look at the archaeology, the etymology and the strategic importance. Wigan's Roman name was Coccium and it was a subordinate garrison to Manchester.

Arthur would have utilised Roman roads to get from Glein to Dubglas. His route would have taken him from Yeavering Bell to the Hadrian's Wall garrison of Carlisle where he may have stopped for reinforcements and supplies. His route then would have been essentially the route the M6 motorway takes now. From Carlisle to Penrith, to Kendal, to Lancaster, to Preston and down to Appley Bridge.

The author at the River Douglas in Appley Bridge

In 1932, a Roman statue was found in Appley Bridge of Cautopates, attendant of Mithras who was a minor god worshipped mostly by Roman soldiers. Evidence suggests Mithras worship in Roman garrisons. Therefore Arthur may have met the Saxons at the banks of the River Douglas in Appley Bridge. Parbold Hill would be of strategic importance – you can see the Welsh hills from there.

If you follow the River Douglas along, we get to Wigan itself. The name Wigan is thought to come from the Saxon 'wig' (battle) hence 'battle town' and archaeology at Parson's Meadow (Highfield Grange) suggests a Dark Age battle (Hardwick 1882, p22). Further along, in Wigan town centre, we come to the historic street the Wiend, which still has an olde world feel with its cobbles and old fashioned architecture.

The River Douglas near the Roman road

In the Wiend, Roman artefacts were found. Wigan Archaeological Society writes:

"It has always been assumed that there was a Roman station at Wigan. Even as early as the beginning of the 19th century the Rev Edmund Sibson suggested it was Coccium, the Roman fort which appears in early Roman literature, and was able to trace three Roman roads leading into Wigan from Warrington, Manchester and Preston. Added to this, many Roman finds have turned up over the years, including funerary vessels from the area of the Gas Works, a Roman altar stone in the Parish Church and many coins and potsherds from around the town centre. However, it was only in the early 1980s, with excavations in the Wiend, that the true nature of Wigan's Roman heritage began to emerge. Two seasons of excavations, by a team from Manchester University, revealed for the first time that Wigan was indeed settled by the Romans and was being used for some kind of industrial activity."

There is also evidence that the soldiers used Darlington Street, down the hill from the main brow of the Wiend, as a cemetery. And in 2005 a Roman bath house was found in the Millgate area. Wigan also has Brythonic place names – such as Bryn (hill) and Ince (Ynys – island) – and in Ince we have what Nennius meant by Linnius. Ince not only has a Celtic name in a town later taken by Saxons, it is also on the route of the Roman roads to Preston and Manchester.

So in Wigan's Douglas we have:
- A town held by Romans and later Saxons
- A town with a River Douglas
- A town of strategic importance leading to Preston and Manchester
- A town where excavations show battles and evidence of Roman garrisons and worship
- A town where the etymology recalls a battle
- Wigan is also close to Martin Mere (Myrddin's Mere) where Lancelot was said to have dwelled (see Pennine Dragon). Some say Linnius is the Saxon word for lake.
- A town within the kingdom of Arthwys ap Mar
- It was of strategic importance and later the site for the famous 'battle of Wigan Lane'

Arthur's Sixth Battle: The battle of Bassas

Rhun simply tells us:
The sixth battle was on the river called Bassas

There have been a number of intelligent suggestions for Bassas including Cambusland in Glasgow, Baschurch in Shropshire and Bass rock in Edinburgh but I would like to propose Bassenthwaite in Cumbria.

Here Arthur could travel directly up the Roman road from Wigan, past Preston and up to the Lake District.

Bassenthwaite Lake

From Dubglas, Arthur must have been returning to Carlisle (taking the proverbial M6 route) which brings him to Bassenthwaite. The area is in the heart of the Celtic kingdom of Rheged, and was said to be the lake Tennyson imaged Excalibur rising from, courtesy of the Lady of the Lake. The aptly-named King Arthur's Round Table is an earthworks at Eamont Bridge, near Penrith.

According to local legends, after Camlan (which I have identified as Camboglanna) Arthur was taken to Avalon (Avalana also on Hadrian's Wall). He was buried underneath Blencathra near Bassenthwaite, which was also the resting place of Avallach. The journey from Camlan to Bassenthwaite would also cross the later site of Pendragon castle and the Eden where Uther Pendragon laid siege. In other words the area is absolutely rich with Arthurian legends.

In 2008 a team of volunteers searching for a lost stone circle and a 14th century castle in Cumbria uncovered what could be a nationally significant Roman encampment, thought to date back to the first century. It was discovered by a team working on the Lake District community project, Bassenthwaite Reflections, at a dig on the Castlerigg prehistoric site near Keswick.

Archaeologist Mark Graham, of Grampus Heritage and Training, said: "In sight of Castlerigg Stone Circle - which was already 3,000 years old at the time of the Roman occupation - the elevated position was strategically well placed for defence. It also has lovely views over Bassenthwaite and to other Roman camps at Troutbeck." The floods which devastated west Cumbria last November have helped rewrite the area's history by unearthing Roman treasures. Work began in a field near Papcastle (which I pointed out in Pennine Dragon may be related to Arthwys' uncle Pabo Post Prydain) in Cockermouth after the floods in 2009 exposed the remains of a settlement.

Mark Graham said: "We are unearthing a site of great historical significance. It is showing the Roman presence in Cockermouth was far more extensive than was believed, with the settlement stretching down to the River Derwent."

The Iron Age Castle How hillfort is located on the summit of Castle How, a rocky hillock rising steeply above the western shore of Bassenthwaite Lake.

- Bassenthwaite was significant to the Romans
- It has a river running into it
- It had an iron age hillfort
- The local area has folklore relating to Arthur and Uther

- It is on a major Roman road between Preston and Carlisle
- It is in the kingdom of Arthwys

Looking at the battles of Nennius we can start to see Arthur's battles emerging. First at Hadrian's Wall, across to Carlisle, down to Dubglas at Coccium and then en route back to Carlisle where he meets the Angles again in the heart of Rheged and engages them at Bassenthwaite water.

Arthur's seventh battle at Celidon

Rhun tells us:
The seventh battle was in the Caledonian Forest, that is, the Battle of Celidon Coit

After Bassas, Arthur has returned to Carlisle and then to his own Hadrianic garrisons, more likely Banna or Camboglanna. His next battle takes him north. It is a convoluted theory that attempts to locate the Caledonian Forest anywhere other than north of the wall. And even today we find the Kielder Forest Park that reaches down to Housesteads Fort on Hadrian's Wall. Housesteads is in the civil parish of Bardon Mill (more on this later) in Northumberland, England, south of Broomlee Lough. The fort was built in stone around AD 124, soon after the construction of the wall began in AD 122 when the area was part of the Roman province of Britannia. Its name has been variously given as Vercovicium, Borcovicus, Borcovicium, and Velurtion.

Hadrian's Wall pictured in 1873

This forest is also listed in the Annales Cambrae. It was the forest that Myrddin fled to after the battle of Arthuret. The Annales record:

"The battle of Arfderydd, between the sons of Eliffer and Gwenddolau son of Ceidio; in which battle Gwenddolau fell; Merlin went mad."

Later we learn that Myrddin ran into the forest where, according to the bards, he could converse with the wildlife.

Here we have:
- A battle clearly established as north of Hadrian's Wall
- A site in the kingdom of Arthwys
- A site connected with Arthwys' grandsons (such as Gwenddolau) and also Myrddin
- A battle site in line with one of the Roman garrisons on Hadrian's Wall.

110

Arthur's eighth battle at Guinnion

Rhun tells us:

"The eighth battle was in Guinnion fort, and in it Arthur carried the image of the holy Mary, the everlasting Virgin, on his shield, and the heathen were put to flight on that day, and there was great slaughter upon them, through the power of Jesus Christ and the power of the holy Virgin Mary, his mother."

The name is very similar to the Roman fort of Vinovium at Binchester, Durham. There was a second place of the same name in the North West - so either way within the kingdom of Arthwys. But in the pattern of battles, the Durham location is the most likely.

Vinovium Roman fort is just over 1 mile (1.6 km) to the north of the town of Bishop Auckland on the banks of the River Wear in County Durham, England.

The fort was probably established around 79 CE to guard the crossing of the River Wear by Dere Street, the main Roman road between York, Hadrian's Wall and Scotland, and also the fort's via principalis. Sitting atop a hill 15 metres above the Wear, Binchester was the largest Roman fort in County Durham. The land was cleared of trees and brush and a huge levelling fill laid down on the plateau before construction of the fort began.

Centuries later, buildings inside the fort were levelled and reconstructed in stone. These included a commandant's house at the heart of the fort and a well-appointed baths building.

A long-term program of excavation begun by the Bowes Museum for Durham County Council ran from 1976–1980, and then again from 1986–1988. It focused primarily upon the baths suite and the attached commandant's house, uncovering several phases of activity.

The first was the construction of the original courtyard house presumably used by the commandant of the fort, built sometime after the middle of the 4th century atop two previous smaller stone buildings, also presumably praetoria. It had attractive decor and was meant for a single occupant. Later, but also perhaps in the 4th century, a detached bath suite was built adjoining the house, necessitating the demolition of part of the earlier building.

It had three rooms: a warm room, a hot room, and a hot room with two plunge baths. The excavators understood this bath building to be for the use of the commandant only. Still later, the house seems to have lost its singular occupant. Rooms were subdivided and several self-contained units were created in what was originally a large house. The baths received a flagstone court, a triple-arched gateway, and a small anteroom, and it is suggested that the reorganisation of both structures meant the baths were opened to the entire regiment at the fort. A coin of the usurper Magnentius, minted between 350 and 360, may provide a terminus post quem for these renovations. The baths and house then fell on rough times. Lack of maintenance of the baths can be seen archaeologically in the next period, and in the house, the rooms come to be used for industry, including blacksmithing, lime slaking, and animal butchery. A midden dug in a channel around most of the building held a great deal of animal bones and debris. Finally, the collapse of a few walls and part of the roof of the baths seems to have heralded the end for the complex some time in the post-Roman period. However, the entire fort seems to have been used as a cemetery from the mid-6th to the 11th centuries. A Saxon woman was found buried in the rubble caused by the roof collapse.

In Guinnion we have:

- Another fortress along Hadrian's Wall
- Within the kingdom of Arthwys
- Used from Roman to Saxon period

Arthur's ninth battle at The City of the Legions

Rhun tell us:

"The ninth battle was at The City of the Legions that is called Caer Leon."

While it is tempting to think the City of the Legion was York, the evidence points towards Chester.

There were two Caerleons – Caerleon-on-Usk and Caerleon-on-Dee which is Chester.

Chester was built on the River Dee, which the Romans called Deva from a Celtic water goddess.

While the Dux commanded from York to Hadrian's Wall, the Count of Britain commanded at Chester. Arthur – it seems - held both positions.

Roman Chester – the City of the Legions

Caerleon (Chester) was linked by road to Badon (Buxton). It was also linked by road to Dubglas (Wigan) and Mamacium, en route to York. From Wigan the road continued up to Tribruit (Ribchester). Both Ribchester and York connected by road to Catterick.

Stoker (1965) wrote: "In the north, at York was the Duke of Britain (Dux Britannianum)....and the western coast was the Comes Britannianum or Count of Britain)... There is little doubt that Chester was the headquarters of the Count of Britain and capital of Britannia Secunda."

In the History of Manchester (1775) Whitaker gives an interesting hypothesis for Arthur's battles. He swaps two battles so that City of the Legions was first and Glein, ninth.

Whitaker's battle hypothesis:

Arthur is sent by Ambrosius to meet the Saxons at Chester, through the Ribble Gap. Arthur defeats them and runs them towards Wigan.

He engages them in four battles on the River Dubglas. He says Wigan means "place of the battles" in Saxon.

Whitaker says Arthur then fought at Pesa (Bassas) in Kendal and then north to Celidon. He then beats the Saxons at Guinnion (Binchester) and Agned (Edinburgh).

Glein becomes Glen in Northumberland and Tribruit, the Ribble.

He states: "The engagement in the Glen could have been held only with those who, being routed in Cheshire, slaughtered in Lancashire and defeated in Cumberland, and the bishopric of Durham, retired into Northumberland."

Of course the only other serious contender for "City of the Legions" is York and since Arthwys was King of York, that eventuality would hardly weaken our case.

A gilded figure of Hercules found at Birdoswald (a few hundred yards from Camlan) dating back to the 2nd century. It is thought to be in tribute to the Emperor Commodus. It is now in the British Museum

Arthur's tenth battle of Tribruit

Rhun wrote:

"The tenth battle was on the bank of the river called Tribruit"

The Welsh poem Pa Gur (Source 8) includes:

*A pierced shield from **Tryfrwyd**;*
And Mabon son of Mellt

Who stained the grass with gore;
And Anwas the Winged,
And Llwych of the Striking Hand,
Who defended Eidyn on the borders.
Its lord sheltered them,
My nephew destroyed them,
Cei pleaded with them
While he slew them three by three.
When Celli was lost
Savagery was experienced.
Cei pleaded with them
While he hewed them down.
Though Arthur was but playing,
Blood was flowing

The interesting thing with these sources is that Rhun (Source 4) and Pa Gur (Source 8) are sources uninfluenced by each other but both include Tribruit/Tryfrwyd. Here it also mentions "Llwych who defended Eidyn" which is of course Arthwys' brother Llaenauc defending Edinburgh, heartland of the Gododdin.

Since we have already identified that the Ribble flows into the Douglas, and the Roman road ran from Preston to Wigan, it makes perfect sense that Tribruit was the Ribble.

Bremetennacum, or Bremetennacum Veteranorum was a Roman fort on the site of the present day village of Ribchester near Preston and the Ribble. The first known Roman activity was the building of a timber fort, believed to have been constructed during the campaigns of Petillius Cerialis around AD 72/3. This was replaced by a stone fort in the 2nd century. For most of its existence the fort was garrisoned by Sarmatian auxiliaries, first stationed in Britain by Marcus Aurelius in 175. Pottery evidence indicates that the fort was occupied for most of the 4th century until the end of the Roman period – or in other words Arthur's time.

Statue excavated at Ribchester

The civilian site outside the fort was extensive and covered an area more or less corresponding to that of the modern village. Narrow plots were occupied perpendicular to the main Roman roads. Excavations have revealed rectangular wooden buildings used as workshops and dwellings. Craftsmen plied their trades in the vicus, providing essential goods for both civilians and military personnel alike. Metalworkers and leather workers were particularly abundant, supplying all kinds of military and cavalry equipment. The vicus was also the site of the baths, the most substantial stone built construction outside the fort, and at least two temples, fulfilling important social and religious functions.

The road network of Roman Lancashire grew around the two main south-north routes, its most important focus being Manchester where at least six roads met – one heading ultimately for Carlisle. Therefore Arthur had a route to return to Hadrian's Wall at Carlisle. The A56 north from Manchester through

118

Prestwich follows the Roman road to Ribchester and Carlisle. Lancashire can offer one of the finest of all views of a Roman road. From Jeffrey Hill above Longridge on a clear day the unerringly straight line of the road from Ribchester to Burrow in Lonsdale is picked out by lanes and hedgerows over into Yorkshire, and on the horizon, peeping over the ridge above Browsholme, is the summit of Pen-y-Ghent, the sighting point used by the Roman surveyors almost two thousand years ago.

The mountains of Whernside (736 m or 2,415 ft), Ingleborough (723 m or 2,372 ft) and Pen-y-ghent (694 m or 2,277 ft) are collectively known as the Three Peaks. The peaks, which form part of the Pennine range, encircle the heads of the valleys of the River Ribble and of Chapel-le-Dale in the Yorkshire Dales National Park in the North of England.

The place-name of the mountain Pen-y-Ghent is included, as it means, '*The Head of Ghent*'. An expression that may indicate that this mountain was on the boundary of a territory called 'Ghent' at some time in the past. In place-name terms, '*Ghent*' in Pen-y-Ghent, is of the same origin as, Ghent in Belgium, Kent in the South East of England and Gwent in South Wales.

This poses the question, did the legends that linked Arthur to Gwent in South Wales, actually occur because Arthur's connections with a 'Ghent' kingdom associated with Pen-y-Ghent, were misappropriated by the bards due to place-name similarity?

Could this be the origin of the Kentishmen?

Rhun writes:

At that time the English increased their numbers and grew in Britain. On Hengest's death, his son Octha came down from the north of Britain to the kingdom of the Kentishmen, and from him are sprung the kings of the Kentishmen. Then Arthur fought against them in those days, together with the kings of the British; but he was their leader in battle. The first battle was at the mouth of the river called Glein. The second, the third, the fourth, and the fifth were on another river, called the Douglas, which is in the country of Lindsey.

Now let's look at the Ribble as Tribruit:

- The Ribble flows into the Douglas, linking the two rivers of Nennius – Tribruit and Dubglas
- The Roman road of Dubglas/Linuis (Ince) runs north to Preston – where the Ribble is. Both Coccium (Wigan) and Ribchester had the kind of forts and infrastructure that a Dux like Arthur would utilise
- Within the kingdom of Arthwys
- Tribruit was attributed to Arthur in two independent sources – Nennius and Pa Gur

Arthur's eleventh battle: Agned or Bregoin

"The eleventh battle was on the hill called Agned"

Or alternatively:

"The eleventh battle was on the Mountain Breguoin, which we call Cat Bregion".

Geoffrey of Monmouth identifies Monte Agned as Edinburgh, and there appears to be little evidence to contradict him. The rock of Edinburgh Castle was certainly occupied at this time. It was a strategic point of some importance at the centre of the Gododdin.

The fort at Bremenium

However another version of the Historia gives this battle the alternative name of Breguoin - this name comes from Bremenium, now High Rochester in Northumberland. That was also the likely site of King Urien Rheged's Battle of the Cells of Brewyn, as mentioned in Welsh poetry.

Arthur's 12th battle at Badon

Gildas tells us:

"From that time, the citizens were sometimes victorious, sometimes the enemy, in order that the Lord, according to His wont, might try in this nation the Israel of to-day, whether it loves Him or not. This continued up to the year of the siege of Badon Hill (obsessionis Badonici montis), and of almost the last great slaughter inflicted upon the rascally crew. And this commences, a fact I know, as the forty-fourth year, with one month now elapsed; it is also my nativity."

Rhun tells us:

"The twelfth battle was on Mount Badon in which there fell in one day 960 men from one charge by Arthur; and no one struck them down except Arthur himself".

The Annales Cambrae tells us:

516AD: "The Battle of Badon, in which Arthur carried the Cross of our Lord Jesus Christ for three days and three nights upon his shoulders and the Britons were the victors".

565AD: "The first celebration of Easter among the Saxons. The second battle of Badon. Morgan dies."

The battle with which Arthur is most synonymous is "Mons Badonicus", a siege or battle listed by Gildas, Nennius and the Annales Cambrae.

We know it was fought after Vortigern's time and before the time of Maelgwyn which gives a range of about 480-540. The Annales Cambrae suggests the date 516 and this seems to work well, although many have suggested a date of about 510 works better.

Badon's most commonly identified locations are Bath and Badbury Rings, but northern locations have also been hypothesised including Dunbarton and Bowden Hill in Scotland.

In Pennine Dragon, I suggested that Bathamgate in Buxton had as much claim to being a potential Badon as Bath, and makes more sense if we accept that Arthwys ap Mar was Arthur.

However, in my travels around Hadrian's Wall I considered another site I now think far more likely - Bardon Mill near Battle Hill in Hexham.

Inscription reads:
THE CROSS WHICH STOOD AT THE HEAD OF THE GRAVE OF
ACCA BISHOP OF HEXHAM AD 709-732 WHO DIED AD 740

The old name of Bardon may be derived from the Saxon word for Bard.

Hadrian's Wall is located three miles north of Bardon Mill and the best preserved Fort is Housesteads, located three miles from the village.

Not only is this location near Hexham in Northumbria perfect because of its placement near other battle sites, it is also of strategic importance and famously has links with a cross being used as a war standard.

A few kilometres from Bardon Bill is the village of Beltingham. The shaft of a Saxon cross sits at the east end of St Cuthbert's church, dated circa AD680, and at the other end of the church yard is an ancient Yew tree.

Carrying the cross into battle

The area was held by the Romans and Britons and then lost to the Saxons. It was home to the Roman garrison of Vindolanda.

The Vindolanda Chraitable Trust writes: "Artefacts such as a 5th/6th century penannular brooch and an Anglo-Saxon strap end dating from the 9th -11th centuries have helped to push the post Roman occupation of the site into covering a longer period than that of the Roman occupation of Vindolanda" - a period that includes the Arthurian age.

And it is not just Arthur that had the cross as his standard. Arthwys' ancestor Constantine the Great had pieces of what he believed to be the true cross. They no doubt played a part in his coronation in York. Could they also have been passed to Arthwys?

On the night of 27th October 312 AD, Constantine the Great, Roman Emperor from 306 to 337, is said to have received his famous 'Vision of the Cross' and his mother Helena was inspired to undertake a journey to the Holy Land in 326-28 in which, according to legend, she is said to have discovered the True Cross.

Crosses and memories of Constantine and Helena remain in the Yorkshire area and the cult of the true cross was strongest there.

Let's imagine Arthur had, on his shoulders, parts of what he believed to be the cross, handed down from Constantine. Could these artefacts then be passed on to the next century?

Certainly the Northumbrian King Oswald erected a wooden cross prior to his victory over Cadwallon at Hefenfelth (Heavenfield), near Hexham, in 633 AD.

St Oswald's cross in Heavenfield

And this shows that not only was the cult of the cross still alive and well, but also of the strategic importance of Hexham in 633, significant because the second battle of Badon was fought in 665. Further evidence of this cross cult can bee seen in the Ruthwell Cross, in Dumfries and Galloway. The Annales Cambrae records:

"The first celebration of Easter among the Saxons. The second battle of Badon. Morgan dies."

Even today the site of the battle of Heavenfield is marked by a cross.

- Bardon, Battle Hill was of strategic importance to the Romans
- The area was lost to the Saxons

- The area was known for the use of the cross as a battle standard
- The area is not only a candidate for an Arthurian Badon, but the battle of Heavenfield shows it was also a candidate for the second Badon.
- It had a Pre-Hadrianic bath house
- Several commanding officers' residences and some barracks
- 3rd and 4th century evidence of civilian houses and workshops, latrines, strong room and a Roman Celtic temple to an unknown God
- Post-Roman mausoleum and Christian church
- Replicas of a Roman temple and shop, a Romano-British house and replica sections of Hadrian's Wall in turf, timber and stone.

Nennius also provides us with a piece of information he got from Source 4, that Arthur was the Dux Bellorum. The Dux was always identified as commanding the 6th legion (York) and stationed at Hadrian's Wall. The Notitia Dignitatum states:

Dux Britanniarum.
Sub dispositione viri spectabilis ducis Britanniarum:
Praefectus legionis sextae.

This translates approximately as "Under the command of the honourable Duke of the Britains, Prefect of the Sixth Legion".

Arthur's Battles contrasted with the kings of the generation. Each of the battle sites are within the territory of Arthwys

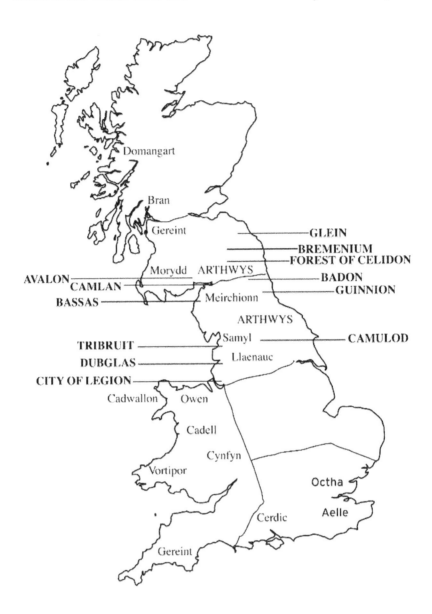

Content of The Lost Book of Arthur by Rhun ap Urien

- Arthwys ap Mar succeeds Ambrosius as Dux Bellorum based at York
- He defeats the Angles at Glein, Northumbria
- He marches down to Wigan where he defeats the Angles at Dubglas
- He marches north to Rheged where he engages the Angles at Bassenthwaite
- He makes for Hadrian's Wall, where he engages the enemy at the Kelder Forest
- He defeats the Angles at Guinnion Fort on Hadrian's Wall
- He marches south and engages the Angles at Chester
- He marches back north and defeats the Angles at Ribchester
- Returning to Northumbria, he engages the Angles at Rochester
- In Arthur's final battle he meets the Angles at Bardon
- After his death Arthur's kingdom is lost to Ida in Northumbria.

The Lost Book of Arthur is essentially a record of Arthwys' victories over the Angles in Northumbria and the defence of the wall.

It supports Gildas' description of Badon (Source 1), it supports Anierin's identification of Arthur as fighting the Angles in the north (Source 2) and it supports Taliesin's identification of Arthur as Guletic of the 'old renowned boundary.'

The Lost Book of Mordred

SOURCE 5: The Lost Book of Mordred

The Lost Book of Mordred is another work that is beyond conjecture. It could be argued that the Annales Cambrae took its reference to Badon from Source 1 (Gildas), or Source 4 (**The Lost Book of Arthur**) but that does not explain the entries on Camlann and Arthuret.

The Camlann entry comes from what we will call the **Lost Book of Mordred** and the Arthuret entry comes from what we will call **The Lost Book of Uther and Merlin.**

Here are entries in the Annales Cambrae which I have annotated. Conventional dating is used.

The Annales

447 Days as dark as night. 453 Easter altered on the Lord's Day by Pope Leo, Bishop of Rome.

454 St. Brigid is born.

457 St. Patrick goes to the Lord.

458 St. David is born in the thirtieth year after Patrick left Menevia.

468 The death of Bishop Benignus.

501 Bishop Ebur rests in Christ, he was 350 years old.

516 The Battle of Badon, in which Arthur carried the Cross of our Lord Jesus Christ for three days and three nights on his shoulders and the Britons were the victors. [This supports both Source 1 and 4]

521 St. Columba is born. The death of St. Brigid.

537 The battle of Camlann, in which Arthur and Medraut fell: and there was plague in Britain and Ireland. [This is the earliest reference to Camlann and Mordred and is not found in Sources 1-4].

544 The sleep [death] of Ciaran.

547 The great death [plague] in which Maelgwn, king of Gwynedd died. Thus they say 'The long sleep of Maelgwn in the court of Rhos'. Then was the yellow plague. [Maelgwyn was referenced in Source 1.]

558 The death of Gabrán, son of Dungart.

562 Columba went to Britain.

565 The voyage of Gildas to Ireland.

569 The 'Synod of Victory' was held between the Britons.

570 Gildas, wisest of Britons, died.

573 The battle of Arfderydd between the sons of Eliffer and Gwenddolau son of Ceidio; in which battle Gwenddolau fell; Myrddin went mad. [Note Eliffer or Eleuther and Ceidio and Keidyaw were the sons of Arthwys. This battle is not mentioned in Sources 1-4]

574 The sleep [death] of Brendan of Birr.

580 Gwrgi and Peredur sons of Elifert died. [Gwrgi and Peredur were grandsons of Arthwys.]

584 Battle against the Isle of Man and the burial of Daniel of the Bangors.

589 The conversion of Constantine [king of Britain] to the Lord.

594 Aethelbert reigned in England.

595 The death of Columba.

The death of king Dunod son of Pabo.

[Note – Pabo was the uncle of Arthwys]

Augustine and Mellitus converted the English to Christ.

601 The synod of Urbs Legionis [Chester].

Gregory died in Christ and also bishop David of Moni Iudeorum.

606 The burial of bishop Cynog.

607 The death of Aidan son of Gabrán. [Note Aidan was the grandson of Domangart and father of Artur of Dalriada.]

612 The death of Kentigern and bishop Dyfrig.

613 The battle of Caer Legion [Chester]. And there died Selyf son of Cynan. And Iago son of Beli slept [died]. [This supports the theory that Source 4's earlier battle at the City of the Legions was Chester.]

616 Ceredig died.

617 Edwin begins his reign.

624 The sun is covered [eclipsed].

626 Edwin is baptised, and Rhun son of Urien baptised him.

[Note this is Rhun who wrote The Lost Book of Arthur]

627 Belin dies.

629 The beseiging of king Cadwallon in the island of Glannauc.

630 Gwyddgar comes and does not return. On the Kalends of January the battle of Meigen; and there Edwin was killed with his two sons; but Cadwallon was the victor.

631 The battle of Cantscaul in which Cadwallon fell.

632 The slaughter of the [river] Severn and the death of Idris.

644 The battle of Cogfry in which Oswald king of the Northmen and Eawa king of the Mercians fell.

645 The hammering of the region of Dyfed, when the monastery of David was burnt. [This may have occurred in the reign of Arthur II of Dyfed]

649 Slaughter in Gwent.

650 The rising of a star.

656 The slaughter of Campus Gaius.

657 Penda killed.

658 Oswy came and took plunder.

661 Cummine the tall died.

662 Brocmail the tusked dies.

665 The first celebration of Easter among the Saxons. The second battle of Badon. Morgan dies. [This could be Morgan, son of Athrwys ap Meurig. Note the Second battle of Badon is not mentioned by Gildas or Nennius.]

The Lost Book of Mordred

If **The Lost Book of Arthur** tells the story of Arthwys ap Mar, then the **Lost Book of Mordred** tells the story of his brother Morydd.

Arthwys and Morydd were the sons of Mar. It is interesting that as Dux, Arthur was associated with Hadrian's Wall and in many legends of Mordred he is also associated with that area and was something of a hero north of the border.

The name Mordred has been suggested as related to Moderatus. August Hunt points this out in his excellent article Glein to Camlann where he says: "we know of a Trajanic period prefect named C. Rufius Moderatus, who left inscriptions at Greatchesters on the Wall and Brough-under-Stainmore in Cumbria."

And this is the key to understanding Mordred. Like his brother Arthur he was stationed at Hadrian's Wall, one as the Dux, one as the Moderatus.

Therefore it makes perfect sense that their final battle, a civil war between two brothers, was also fought at Hadrian's Wall and the location of course was Camboglanna.

Centuries later, Morydd was confused with the later Welsh prince Medraut and he was given that spelling as his name in the Annales Cambrae and Camlann was transported as far south as Slaughter Bridge in Cornwall.

We can suggest that The Lost Book of Mordred includes some information on Arthur's previous conflicts, but unlike The Lost Book of Arthur, it does not bother to cite the first 11 battles, only Badon.

From Sources 1-4 we know that Arthur was born in around 470 and took the fight to the Angles in the early 6th Century. Now The Lost Book of Mordred tells us he faced civil war later.

In around 520-537 Arthur was challenged by his own brother. If the dates are correct, in 537 Arthur was 67 year old and had delivered 20 years of peace from the Saxons.

The wall had been the stronghold of Coel, Ceneu, Mar and Arthur, and it was known as the seat of the Guletic (Gwledig/warleader).

For Mordred to challenge Arthur on his home territory showed great confidence, or perhaps Arthur's troops were scattered, fighting Cerdic in the south.

The first mention of the Camboglanna fort is contained within the Notitia Dignitatum, the 'Register of Dignitaries' of the late-4th/early-5th centuries. In this document, the Birdoswald fort or the next one along at Castlesteads - is listed as Amboglanna, between the entries for Magnis (Carvoran, Northumberland) and Petrianis (Stanwix, Cumbria).

The fort is also mentioned in the seventh century Ravenna Cosmology, where it is seemingly listed twice; the first and most likely entry is named Gabaglanda, and occurs between Magnis (Carvoran, Northumberland) and Vindolande (Chesterholm, Northumberland), whereas the second entry, Cambroianna, is listed between the unidentified stations Locatreve and Smetri.

Coventina's Well

The accepted name Camboglanna is Celtic in origin and translates as 'the Crooked Glen', which refers, no doubt, to the fort's spectacular southern aspect overlooking a convoluted meander of the River Irthing, towards the Roman signal station at Upper Denton on the Stanegate.

It has been theorised recently that Irthing could be derived from the name Arthwys.

Augustus Hunt, who identifies Arthur with the son of Arthwys ap Mar (Keidyaw), states: "In considering Arthwys as an ancestor of Arthur, and noting that the River Irthing does indeed fulfill the requirements of being at a sort of hub of all the other tribal territories designated by eponyms in the genealogies, I would put forward the idea that both the Irth and Irthing rivers do indeed preserve a "bear" name.

"arth has been invoked by Breeze, and, while I'm pretty sceptical, a form *erth-in with internal i-affection would be a possible early river-name, 'little bear' or (as -inn was not necessarily diminutive) 'bear stream'."

Birdoswald stands high above a meander in the River Irthing, in one of the most picturesque settings on Hadrian's Wall. A Roman fort, turret and milecastle can all be seen on this excellent stretch of the Wall.

With probably the best-preserved defences of any Wall fort, this was an important base for some 1,000 Roman soldiers, succeeding an earlier fort of turf and timber. The section of Wall to the east, also of stone replacing turf, is the longest continuous stretch visible today.

Archaeological discoveries over the past 150 years have revealed a great deal about Roman military life at Birdoswald. Three of the four main gateways of the fort have been unearthed, as have the outside walls, two granary buildings, workshops and a unique drill hall.

People continued to live at Birdoswald after the Roman withdrawal. In the 5th century a large timber hall was built over the collapsed Roman granaries, perhaps for a local British chieftain. Later, a medieval tower house was raised here, replaced in the 16th century by a fortified 'bastle' farmhouse designed to protect its inhabitants from the notorious 'Border Reivers'.

The Birdoswald Visitor Centre provides a good introduction to Hadrian's Wall, and tells the intriguing story of Birdoswald and the people who have lived here over the past 2,000 years. When I visited I observed part of it was listed as being used in 520AD – Arthur's flourit.

The Lady of the Lake, Avalon and Camlan

In Arthurian legend, Excalibur was thrown in the water for Vivianna (the Lady in the Lake). The real Vivianna (not to be confused with St Nyfaine the real Nimue) was the goddess Covianna or Coventina.

Roman and British soldiers would throw swords and coins as offerings to her. And if Arthur was mortally wounded and gave up his sword at Camboglanna, then Coventina's well nearby would be the fitting location.

Coventina was a Romano-British goddess of wells and springs. She is known from multiple inscriptions at one site in the Northumberland County of the United Kingdom, an area surrounding a wellspring near Carrawburgh on Hadrian's Wall.

Dedications to Coventina and votive deposits were found in a walled area which had been built to contain the outflow from a spring now called "Coventina's Well". The well and the walled area surrounding it are nearby the site variously referred to as Procolita, Brocolitia, or Brocolita, once a Roman fort and settlement on Hadrian's Wall, now known as Carrawburgh.

Excavation also revealed a large quantity of coinage, from early Augustan coins to those of the late 4th century, and other votive objects such as brooches, rings, pins, glassware, and pottery. These are assumed to be votive offerings due to the quantity discovered in a single location. One inscription reads: "To Coventina, I Aelius Tertius, prefect of the First Cohort of the Batavi, willingly and deservedly fulfils a vow." Another, according to Arthurian author Graham Phillips, reads: "To the goddess Coventina, the first cohort of Cugerni… willingly placed this offering." Another reads: "For the goddess Coventina, Crotus and his freedmen, fulfil [their vow] for the health of the soldiers." There is no question that the men of Hadrian's Wall gave offerings to Coventina. This could easily equate to them later making offerings to, let's say, Viviana.

Camlann is mentioned in Culhwch and this too suggests that The Lost Book of Mordred must have been one of the sources for the story. It states:

Morvran the son of Tegid (no one struck him in the battle of Camlan by reason of his ugliness; all thought he was an auxiliary devil. Hair had he upon him like the hair of a stag). And Sandde Bryd Angel (no one touched him with a spear in the battle of Camlan because of his beauty; all thought he was a ministering angel). And Kynwyl Sant (the third man that escaped from the battle of Camlan, and he was the last who parted from Arthur on Hengroen his horse). The sons of Llwch Llawwynnyawg (from beyond the raging sea). Llenlleawg Wyddel, and Ardderchawg Prydain. Cas the son of Saidi, Gwrvan Gwallt Avwyn, and Gwyllennhin the king of France, and Gwittart the son of Oedd king of Ireland, Garselit Wyddel, Panawr Pen Bagad, and Ffleudor the son of Nav, Gwynnhyvar mayor of

Cornwall and Devon (the ninth man that rallied the battle of Camlan).

Here it seems to confirm that Culhwch borrowed from two sources –

The Lost Book of Llaenauc that identifies Arthur's wife as Cywair

The Lost Book of Mordred that says the male mayor of Cornwall and Devon was called Gwynnhyvar, and he caused the battle of Camlan.

Here it seems likely that the author of Culhwch confused the two and Cywair ended up being called Gwenhwyfar, when actually that was the name of the man who caused Camlan.

Content of the Lost Book of Mordred

• Arthwys and his brother Morydd defeat the Angles at Badon in 516AD
• Morydd rebels against Arthwys and they clash at Camboglanna
• Arthwys is fatally wounded
• Arthwys instructs that his sword is thrown into Coventina's Well
• Arthwys is succeeded by his son Keidyaw
• Morydd is succeeded by his son Madog

SOURCE 6: The Lost Book of Llaenauc

Llaenauc is the basis for King Arthur's champion Lleminawc, who was in turn the basis for the stories of Lancelot. Llaenauc's son Gwallawg is the basis for Galahad. Therefore they are very significant.

Guallauc ap (son of) Llaenauc was an important king in late sixth-century Britain, and may have ruled the kingdom of Elmet. What do we know about him?

He features in king lists:

[G]uallauc map Laenauc map Masguic clop map Ceneú map Coyl hen
-Harleian genealogies
Gwallawc m lyeynac m mar m coyl hen.
-Jesus College genealogy

Both genealogies stop at Guallauc and do not list any descendants. He features in Welsh Triads:

Three Adulterers' Horses of the Island of Britain:
Fferlas [Grey Fetlock] horse of Dalldaf son of Cunin, and Gwelwgan Gohoewgein horse of Caradawg son of Gwallawc, and Gwrbrith [Spotted Dun] horse of Rahawd.

Three Pillars of Battle of the Island of Britain:
Dunawd son of Pabo Pillar of Britain, and Gwallawg son of Lleenawg, and Cynfelyn the Leprous
Taliesin (Source 3) cities him:
He will judge all, the supreme man. With his will as a judge; and let him be benefited
And he is mentioned in The Lost Book of Arthur (Source 4) by Rhun which was later used by Nennius:

Adda, son of Ida, reigned eight years; Ethelric, son of Adda, reigned four years. Theodoric, son of Ida, reigned seven years. Freothwulf reigned six years. In whose time the kingdom of Kent, by the mission of Gregory, received baptism. Hussa reigned seven years. Against him fought four kings, Urien, and Ryderthen, and Guallauc, and Morcant. Theodoric fought bravely, together with his sons, against that Urien.

The first element of the name Guallauc means 'wall', so Guallauc may mean something like 'man of the wall'. This immediately calls to mind the two Roman walls in what is now northern England (Hadrian's Wall) or southern Scotland (the Antonine Wall) but he may have also ruled as far south as Elmet (Leeds). Llaenauc and Gwallawg are therefore about as well established in history as it gets. We know that Llaenauc was Arthwys' brother and we know he was succeeded by his great warrior son Gwallawg, but what else do we know?

• Arthwys and Llaenauc also had a brother called Einion. As I pointed out in Pennine Dragon, he is best known for falling in love with a girl called Olwen. The story 'Einion and Olwen' is a traditional Welsh tale, the best known version of which is Culhwch and Olwen.

• Arthwys' wife Cywair was Irish. Therefore either he met her in Britain or he met her in Ireland. The latter is most likely. So at some point Arthwys and his retinue crossed the Irish sea.

Mythical Lancelot of Dolorous Garde

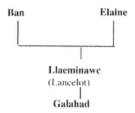

Historic Llaenauc of Din Garde

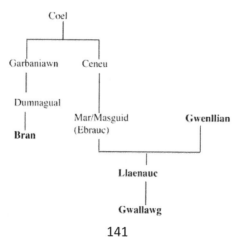

At some point the story of Arthwys, Einion, Llaenauc, Cywair and Olwen became infused with Gaelic mythology full of questing beasts, magical journeys and special swords. And much like Einion's quest for Olwen, it seems at some point Arthwys and Llaenauc had to rescue Cywair from the clutches of either Morydd or Maelgwyn.

The Lost Book of Llaenauc also influenced the work of Chretian de Troyes, and if anybody doubts that Chretien had access to a northern chronicle – consider that two of his main subjects were Owain ap Urien and Peredur of York!

This is significant because it shows that Chretien, like Geoffrey had access to a Northern Chronicle (why else would he write about Owain and Peredur?) and it is from this Northern Chronicle he derived his story of Lancelot from Llaenauc, infused with the Irish legends of Lugh.

SOURCE 7: The Lost Book of Uther
Ystoria Britanica

Geoffrey of Monmouth claims that in writing his History of the Kings of Britain he translated 'a very old book in the British tongue' (Britannici sermonis librum uetustissimum). Many have assumed that this book was Gildas (Source 1) or Nennius since many of his characters are drawn from those works, including Vortigern, Ambrosius and Arthur.

Geoffrey also takes characters and themes from Welsh mythology. Some of the narrative, particularly Arthur's conquest of Europe, seems to be drawn from Culhwch.

However there is one notable aspect of Geoffrey's work not found in Gildas, Nennius, the Annales Cambrae or Culhwch and that is Arthur succeeding his father Uther.

Many have claimed that Geoffrey simply invented Uther by misunderstanding the phrase Arthur mab Uter, but that does not wash because Uther was well recorded in Welsh mythology, including by Taliesin.

The second problem is that we know Geoffrey must have had access to a northern chronicle, because he tells the story of Artegal (Arthwys), Peredur and Eleuther. Geoffrey misidentifies them in history but from what we know of Northern king lists, he must have had access to chronicles that mention them.

Somehow Geoffrey knew that Uther was Arthur's father – and that Uther fought around York. He knew that Arthur was crowned in York, and he knew that Arthur (or at least Arthwys who he calls Artegal) was related to Eleuther and Peredur.

Geoffrey was clearly not lying about possessing this chronicle.

We know that the chronicle must have included:

- Mar (Uther I) succeeding Ambrosius and their father 'Constantine'
- Uther fighting in York
- Uther winning victories in Britanny and Gaul
- Arthur succeeding Uther and being crowned in York
- Arthur winning victories in Britanny and Gaul
- Arthur being succeeded by Eleuther (Uther II)
- Eleuther being succeeded by Peredur (Retheior-Uther III)

Uther, calling together the clergy of the country, took upon him the crown of the island, and with universal assent was raised to be King. And, remembering in what wise Merlin had interpreted the meaning of the star aforementioned, bade two dragons be wrought in gold in the likeness of the dragon he had seen upon the ray of the star. And when that they had been wrought in marvellous cunning craftsmanship, he made offering of the one unto the chief church of the See of Winton, but the other did he keep himself to carry about with him in the wars. From that day forth was he called Uther Pendragon, for thus do we call a dragon's head in the British tongue. And the reason wherefore this name was given unto him was that Merlin had prophesied he should be King by means of the dragon...

Geoffrey introduces Uther with the surname Pendragon. It is tempting to think that this was entirely because of Nennius' story of the boy Emrys telling Vortigern about the battling dragons beneath the castle. But Uther Pendragon does appear in his own right in Welsh tradition.

In the 'Dialogue of Arthur and the Eagle', the eagle reveals itself to be Arthur's deceased nephew, Eliwlod son of Madawg son of Uthyr (stanzas 7-9), i.e. Arthur and Madog are both sons of Uthyr.

Pa Gur mentions Uther Pendragon:

"Mabon, the son of Modron, The servant of Uthyr Pendragon."

Octa, accordingly, having surrounded him with a passing great army, did invade the Northern provinces, nor did he stint to give his cruelty free course until he had destroyed all the cities and strong places from Albany as far as York. At last, when he had begun to beleaguer that city, Uther Pendragon came upon him with the whole force of the kingdom and gave him battle. The Saxons stood their ground like men, remaining unbroken by the assaults of the Britons, who were forced at last to flee..

It is clear here that Geoffrey's source shows Uther Pendragon fighting in York – and at the time, around 465AD, the king of York was none other than Mar.

The Saxons followed up the victory they had won, and pursued the Britons as far as Mount Damen, when the daylight failed them. Now this hill was steep, and at the top was a hazel coppice, but half-way up were tall broken rocks amongst which wild beasts might well make their lairs.

Mythical King Arthur and his kin

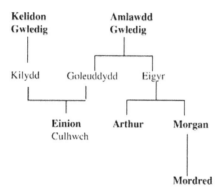

Historic King Arthwys and his kin

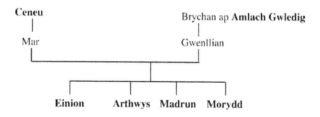

Mike Ashley suggests that Mount Damen was Damems in Keighley, Airedale, about 40 miles from York. Welsh monk Madoc in 1300 stated that Mount Damen however is Wingates, presumably equating it with Windygates Hill in Northumberland. This is nearby to the Roman fort of Brenenium, High Rochester. In any case, once again we see Uther – which let's remember is Iubher/Ebrauc/York – fighting the Angles in the North. He can be none other than King Mar of Ebrauc.

When the Bear began to turn her chariot as it drew toward dawn, Uther bade call the earls and princes to treat with him in counsel how they might best fall upon the enemy....

Here Geoffrey seems to be quoting Gildas, who refers to Cuneglas as Charioteer to the Bear's Stronghold.

After this victory Uther marched unto the city of Alclud, and made ordinance for settling that province, as well as for restoring peace everywhere. He also went round all the nations of the Scots, and made that rebellious people lay aside their savage ways, for such justice did he execute throughout the lands as never another of his predecessors had ever done before him. In his days did misdoers tremble, for they were dealt punishment without mercy. At last, when he had stablished his peace in the parts of the North, he went to London and bade that Octa and Eosa should be kept in prison there...

Here Uther (Ebrauc) is seen conquering Alclud. Let's look at an earlier reference:

Ebraucus also founded the city of Alclud over in Albany; and the castle of Mount Agned, which is now called the Maidens' Castle and the Dolorous Mountain.

This shows Geoffrey was working from a reference where Uther is called Ebraucus. He then confuses Eleuther (Uther II) and his

father Arthwys (who he calls Archgallo) and his brother Peredur, with much earlier rulers.
He records:

When Elidurus [note – this is Eleuther ap Arthwys] had been King for some five years, he came upon his deposed brother one day when he was hunting in the Forest of Calaterium.... The moment he saw him, Elidurus ran up to him, embraced him and kissed him repeatedly. When he had spent some time lamenting the misery to which Archgallo [note – this is Arthwys] was reduced, Elidurus took him to one of his cities called Alclud and there he hid him in his own bedroom. He then pretended to be ill and sent messengers through the kingdom for a whole year to request the princes under his jurisdiction to come to visit him. They all assembled in the town where he lay and he ordered them each in turn to come into his bedroom without making a sound..

Geoffrey records Uther's death:

After the death of Uther Pendragon, the barons of Britain did come together from the divers provinces unto the city of Silchester, and did bear on hand Dubricius, Archbishop of the City of Legions, that he should crown as king Arthur, the late King's son...

This is not the first time Uther is referenced as the father of Arthur. The Book of Taliesin poem Marwnat vthyr pen Uthyr says: "I have shared my refuge, a ninth share in Arthur's valour", and later that "The world would not exist if it were not for my progeny" indicating he has passed on his qualities (or his kingdom) to Arthur.

In the Book of Taliesin there is an elegy entitled Marwnat Uthyr Pen and we should note it has Mar Uthyr Dragon in a gloss in the margin.

It includes the lines:

It is I who broke a hundred fortified towns
It is I who killed a hundred mayors of strongholds
It is I who gave out a hundred cloaks
It is I who cut off a hundred heads.

From his various epithets - Uthyr, Iubher, Uther Pendragon, Mor, Morvawr, Mar Uthyr Dragon - what it appears we have is a series of nicknames and honourary titles. It would appear the man's actual real name was Masguid.

While in the lineage that shows Peredur, Eleuther and Arthwys he is called Mar:
Gwrgi & Phered meibon Eliffer Gosgord Uawr m. Arthwys m.
Mar m. Keneu m. Coel

In the lineage of Llaenauc and Gwallawg he is called Masguic Glop:
[G]uallauc map Laenauc map Masguic clop map Ceneú map
Coyl hen

Who was Uther in mythology?

- Uthyr Pendragon succeeded his father Custennin and brother Emrys. He was the mythical father of Arthur Pendragon.
- He is thought to have conceived Arthur by sleeping with Igrainne, the wife of Gorlois who ruled in King Mark's country.
- He is also listed as Iubher which means Yew [tree].

Who was the real Uther?

- Mar succeeded his father Ceneu and brother Pabo. He was the father of Arthur Penuchel.
- He conceived Arthur by sleeping with Gwenllian, who lived in the same kingdom as Gorlais who ruled in King Meirchionn's

country.

- He came from Ebrauc which means Yew [tree].

The later Uthers

Uther's grandson was Eleuther of Ebrauc. In this name we see the name Ele**uther** and also the name Iubher within the city of Ebrauc. Eleuther was succeeded in Ebrauc (York) by Peredur – the Sir Perceval of legend.

In Dyfed, Peredur was known as Pedr and was succeeded by his son King Arthur II. To the Irish Arthur Mac Retheior – recorded in Scotland as Arthur Mac Iubher.

Therefore the lineage is as follows:

Mar (Mor, Morvawr, Mor Iubher, Mor Uther) circa 445
Arthwys (Arthur Penuchel, King Arthur) Born circa 470
Eleuther (Eliffer, Uther II, Llacheu,) Born circa 500
Peredur (Pedr, Perceval, Retheior, Uther III) circa 540
Arthur (Arthur of Dyfed, King Arthur II) Born Circa 560

Lineage of the House of Ebrauc

1. Coel Hen
2. Ceneu (Vortigern Vortineu)
3. Mar
4. Arthwys
5. Eleuther and Keidyaw
6. Peredur

Lineage of the House of Dyfed

1. Agricola (Possibly identical with Coel Hen)
-
3. Erbin (served Uther)
4. Vortipor (Possibly Gereint. Served Arthur)
5. Congair (Possibly Keidyaw, Cador of Dumnonia)
6. Pedr (Retheior, Uther II, possibly Peredur of York)
7. Arthur II

Lineage of the House of Dumnonia

3. Erbin, Morvawr (Erbin, commander of Mar)
4. Gereint, Arthur (Gereint, commander of Arthur)
5. Cador (Possibly identical of Keidyaw, Congair)
6. Peredur (Possibly Peredur of Ebrauc, Pedr of Dyfed)

SOURCE 8: The Lost Book of Pa Gur

Pa Gur is an incomplete Middle Welsh Arthurian poem in the Black Book of Carmarthen. I refer to it as a 'lost book' because much of it is missing and that which remains is hard to decipher.

It is regarded here as a primary source, because it introduces characters that we later meet in greater detail. Cei and Bedwyr are introduced in Pa Gur, they are later expanded upon in in Culhwch and Geoffrey and ultimately they become the knights Sir Kay and Sir Bedevere.

Pa Gur presents a dialogue between Arthur and Glewlwyd the gate-keeper, followed by a lengthy monologue in which Arthur boasts of his splendid retinue of heroes, above all Kei, in order that they may gain access to some unspecified hall. In Culhwch Glwelwyd is Arthur's gatekeeper so in this way, Culhwch is a kind of sequel to Pa Gur.

The basic structure of one or several heroes seeking admittance to a hall through a series of boasts extolling his/their deeds and qualities has parallels elsewhere in early Welsh and Irish literature.

The poem opens with Arthur and his companion Kei asking about the identity of the gate-keeper (porthawr), who reveals that his name is Glewlwyd Gafaelfawr ("Mighty-Grasp").

Culhwch gets past Arthur's gatekeeper

When Arthur declares that he has the best of heroes with him, Glewlwyd does not allow them inside unless their worth has been established one way or another.

This brief conversation is the starting point for a monologue uttered by Arthur, which takes up the greater part of the poem.
Pa Gur mentions Uther Pendragon: "Mabon, the son of Modron, The servant of Uthyr Pendragon."

The Battle of Tribruit is mentioned: "Did not Manawyd bring perforated shields from Trywruid? And Mabon, the son of Mellt, Spotted the grass with blood?"

Llwch is identified as a guardian of Hadrian's Wall based around Edinburgh, supporting his identification with Llanauc: "And Llwch Llawynnog - Guardians were they On Eiddyn Cymminog, A chieftain that patronised them."

Kay was also fighting in Edinburgh: "Cai, as long as he hewed down. Arthur distributed gifts, The blood trickled down. In the hail of Awarnach, Fighting with a hag, He cleft the head of Paiach. In the fastnesses of Dissethach, In Mynyd Eiddyn."

Cynvyn is mentioned. Is this Arthur's son Cynvelyn? "He contended with Cynvyn."

Bedevere is also mentioned, again fighting at Tribruit: "By the hundred there they fell, There they fell by the hundred, Before the accomplished Bedwyr. On the strands of Trywruid, Contending with Garwlwyd."
Bedevere and Kay are identified as commanders of 900 men, defeating 600, comparable to Nennius's record of Arthur killing 900: "Brave was his disposition, With sword and shield; Vanity were the foremost men Compared with Cai in the battle. The sword in the battle

Was unerring in his hand. They were stanch commanders of a legion for the benefit of the country - Bedwyr and Bridlaw; Nine hundred would to them listen; Six hundred gasping for breath Would be the cost of attacking them."

Emrys also seems to be mentioned: "Servants I have had, Better it was when they were. Before the chiefs of Emrais."
The poem records the deaths of Cai and Llacheu, who we have identified with Cadwallon and Eleuther.

"There was no day that would satisfy him. Unmerited was the death of Cai. Cai the fair, and Llachau, Battles did they sustain,
Before the pang of blue shafts. In the heights of Ystavingon Cai pierced nine witches. Cai the fair went to Mona,

To devastate Llewon. His shield was ready Against Oath Palug When the people welcomed him. Who pierced the Cath Palug? Nine score before dawn

Would fall for its food. Nine score chieftains..."

Photograph of the Vortipor stone taken by the author

SOURCE 9: Llywarch Hen

Llywarch Hen was another Northern British bard like Anierin and Taliesin, and another relation of Arthwys.

His genealogy is:

Llywarch Hen m Elidyr Lydanwyn m Meirchavn m Gorust Ledlvm m Keneu m Coel

Therefore, like Arthur, he was descended from Ceneu ap Coel. It makes perfect sense again that the Arthur he was writing about was Arthwys. Llywarch wrote an Elegy for Gereint. It is long assumed to be about Gereint of Dumnonia (ie Devon) featuring the battle of Llongborth (in this case Portsmouth) but as we have seen there was a Gereint in Scotland too, and Guartepir (Vortipor) of Dyfed had a very similar ancestry pedigree to Gereint of Dumnonia. So when the poem mentions Gereint of Dyvnaint it could equally be Dyfed. In any case, Llywarch mentions Arthur in the poem.

In Llongborth I saw spurs,
And men who did not flinch from the dread of the spears,
Who drank their wine from the bright glass.
In Llongborth I saw the weapons,
Of men, and blood fast dropping,
After the war cry, a fearful return.

In Llongborth I saw Arthur's
Heroes who cut with steel.
The Emperor, ruler of our labour.
In Llongborth Geraint was slain,
A brave man from the region of Dyvnaint,
And before they were overpowered, they committed slaughter.

SOURCE 10: The King Lists

The King Lists are an interesting source for us because they are our best way of dating the historic kings and working out what kingdoms they ruled. Some genealogies must be taken with a pinch of salt, as they stretch back to antiquity, but they also include quality historic records. Here are some of the most significant:

Gwynedd:
This shows the descent of the Kings of Gwynedd from the Gododdin.
[O]uen map [H]iguel map catell map Rotri map mermin map etthil merch cinnan map rotri map Iutguaul map Catgualart map

Catgollaun map Catman map Iacob map Beli map Run map **Mailcun map Catgolaun Iauhir map Eniaun girt map Cuneda map Ætern map Patern pesrut** map Tacit map Cein map Guorcein map doli map Guordoli map dumn map Gurdumn map Amguoloyt map Anguerit map Oumun map dubun map Brithguein map Eugein map Aballac map Amalach, qui fuit beli magni filius et Anna mater eius quam dicunt esse consobrina MARIÆ uirginis matris d'ni n'ri ih'u xp'i.

Note: Mailcun is better known as Maelgwyn, Catgolaun as Cadwallon, Eniaun girt as Einion Yrth, and so on.

Dyfed:

[O]uein map elen merc Ioumarc map Himeyt map Tancoyslt merc ouein map margetiut map Teudos map Regin map Catgocaun map Cathen map **Cloten map Nougoy map Arthur map Petr map Cincar map Guortepir map Aircol** map Triphun map Clotri map Gloitguin map Nimet map dimet map Maxim gulecic map Protec map Protector map Ebiud map Eliud map Stater map Pincr misser map Constans map Constantini magni map Constantíí et helen luicdauc que de Britannia exiuit ad crucem xp'i querendam usque ad ierusalem et inde attulit secum usque ad constantinopolin, et est ibi usque in hodiernum diem.

Note: In the section highlighted, the Arthur is Arthur II of Dyfed born in around 560AD. His grandfather Guortepir is the Vortipor of Gildas (Source 1).

Rheged (Harleian manuscript):

[U]rbgen map Cinmarc map Merchianum map Gurgust map Coilhen.

Note: Urbgen as Urien, Coilhen is Coel Hen.

Rheged (Gwyr y Gogledd manuscript)

Vryen uab Kynuarch m Meirchavn m Gorust Letlvm m Keneu m Coel

Note: The two manuscripts for Rheged match entirely.

Rheged 2 (Gwyr y Gogledd)
Llywarch Hen m Elidyr Lydanwyn m Meirchavn m Gorust Ledlvm m Keneu m Coel
Note: This is a different Elidyr (Eleuther) to the one who was father of Peredur of York.

Elmet (or alternatively Lothian):
[G]uallauc map Laenauc map Masguic clop map Ceneú map Coyl hen
Note: Guallauc and Llaenauc are our 'Galahad and Lancelot' Masguic clop (or Masguid Gloff) is Mar (our Uther Pendragon)

Pennines:
[D]unaut map pappo map Ceneu map Coylhen.
Note: Pappo is Pabo Post Prydain, the brother of Masguic/Mar in the pedigree above.

Pennines 2:
[C]atguallaun liu map Guitcun map Samuil pennissel map Pappo post priten map Ceneu map Gyl hen.
Note: Here we see Pabo Post Prydain, again listed as the son of Ceneu, son of Coel.

Pennines (Gwyr y Gogledd):
Dunavt a Cherwyd a Sawyl Pen Uchel meibyon Pabo Post Prydein m Arthwys m Mar m Keneu m Coel.
Note: Here Arthwys is correctly listed as son of Mar son of Ceneu son of Coel, but Pabo is mistakenly listed as his son, instead of his uncle.

York:
[G]urci ha Peretur mepion eleuther cascord maur map letlum map Ceneú map Coylhen.
Note: Here we see Peredur, son of Eleuther, we then see a garbled reference to Eleuther's grandfather Mar which then lists him as a son of [Gurgust] Ledlum, son of Ceneu, son of Coel. Actually Mar was son of Ceneu.

York (Gwyr y Gogledd):
Gvrgi a Pheredur meibon Eliffer Gosgorduavr m Arthwys m Mar m Keneu m Coel
Note: This genealogy correctly shows Peredur son of Eleuther son of Arthwys son of Mar son of Ceneu son of Coel.

York 2 (Gwyr y Gogledd)
Gwendoleu a Nud a Chof meibyon Keidyav m Arthwys m Mar m Keneu m Coel
Note: This genealogy correctly shows Gwendollau son of Keidyaw son of Arthwys son of Mar son of Ceneu son of Coel

Gwent:
[I]udhail map atroys map Fernmail map Iudhail map Morcant map Atroys [map Mouric] map Teudubric.
Note: Here we see Athrwys (our Arthur III) listed as Atroys.

Summing up the Primary Sources

Source 1   Gildas   C550AD
Gildas introduces Vortigern, Ambrosius, 'The Bear" and the British fight against the Saxons including at Badon.

Source 2   Aneirin   C580AD
Anierin introduces Arthur as a Northern British warleader who fought the Angles

Source 3   Taliesin   C600AD
Taliesin introduces Arthur as Guletic at Hadrian's Wall and also the likes of Uther as well as northern historical kings like Urien, Owain and Gwallawg.

Source 4   Rhun   C600AD
'The Lost Book of Arthur'
Introduces Arthur's rank as Dux Bellorum and that he led the kings of Britain against the Angles in 12 battles culminating in Badon.

Source 5
'The Lost Book of Mordred'
Records Arthur and Morydd fighting each other at Camlann (Camboglanna, at Hadrian's Wall) 20 years after Badon.

Source 6
'The Lost Book of Llaenauc'
Records the adventures of Arthur and his brothers Llaenauc and Einion, and meeting Arthur's wife Cywair in Ireland and the abduction of Cywair by Maelgwyn or Morydd.

Source 7
'The Lost Book of Uther' Ystoria Britanica
Ystoria Britanica records Uther (Mar) succeeding Ambrosius, Arthur's coronation in York and the succession to the kingship of York by Eleuther and Peredur. Records Myrddin fleeing after the battle of Arthuret.

Source 8
'The Lost Book of Pa Gur'
References the battles of Tribruit and Agned, found in Source 4, references Uther found in Source 7, and introduces Arthur's comrades Kei and Bedwyr. Only half of this poem survives.

Source 9   Llywrch Hen 600AD
In the "Elegy for Gereint", Llywarch calls Arthur "imperator", a title meaning emperor, and again suggesting he was senior to kings. Llywarch was a friend of Anierin.

Source 10   The King lists
These genealogies are a goldmine of information. The ones that concern us include The Gwyr y Gogledd and the Harleian. They show the descent of men like Arthwys, Mar, Peredur, Eleuther, Pabo, Urien and Cunedda.

Arthur of Dyfed lived two generations too late to be King Arthur and Athrwys of Gwent even later. From the king lists we may conclude that the only Arthur who lived at the right time to be King Arthur was Arthwys.

What we know of King Arthur from the Primary sources

He was a valiant warrior in battles against the Angles, remembered by the men of the North whose bravery could not compare to his (*Source 2*). He was known as The Bear (Arth) and a young Cuneglas followed him (*Source 1*).

He was the Guletic (commander) at Hadrian's Wall (*Source 3*) and held the title Dux Bellorum (*Source 4*). His father was known as Utherpendragon or Iubher who fought in York (*Source 3, Source 7*). His kinsmen were Einion, Lleminig, Caradoc and Mordred (*Source 5, 6, 7*). His wife Gwenhwyfar was associated with Ireland (*Source 6*). He defeated the Angles in 12 Battles mostly around Hadrian's Wall and across Rheged (*Source 4, Source 8*). His last battle was against his brother Mordred at Camboglanna (*Source 5*). He was succeeded by Eleuther and he by Peredur (*Source 7*). Peredur fought his cousins for Arthur's crown at Arthuret where Myrddin was present.

Contrast with Arthwys ap Mar:

Ruled on the frontline of Angle invasion
Ruled throughout the North
Was also listed as Arthur Penuchel
Was a cousin of Cuneglas
Commanded around Hadrian's Wall
His father ruled in York (Ebrauc)
His brothers were Einion, Llaenauc, Cerdic and Morydd
His wife Cywair was Irish
He ruled around Rheged
He ruled the area around Camboglanna
His son Eleuther, and his son Peredur succeeded him

Timeline derived from Primary sources and king lists

465AD: Mor (Morvidus, Morvawr, Vortimer, Mor Uver) becomes king of York (Ebrauc, Iubher) defeats the Angles and takes the title Uther Pendragon. He marries Gwenllian whose father is Brychan ap Amlach Gwledig.

470AD: Arthur is born. He grows up with his brothers Cerdic, Einion, Llaenauc and Morydd

485AD: Arthur is crowned in York. His coronation is attended by his cousin Dunaut and his elderly grandfather Ceneu. His first skirmish is also in York. The next garrison along is Camulod.

489AD: Arthur is summoned to Hadrian's Wall where he is appointed Dux Bellorum. He defeats the Angles at Glein.

492AD: Arthur marches south and engages the Angles in four battles at the River Douglas in Coccium.

495AD: Arthur marches back north towards Hadrian's Wall and, stopping at Papcester, he engages the Angles at Bassenthwaite.

498AD: Returning to Hadrian's Wall Arthur engages the Angles at the Kielder Forest

500AD: Arthur's bastard son Cinbelin is born

501AD: Arthur engages the Angles at Vinovium

504AD: Arthur and his brothers Einion and Llaenauc move south and sail over to Ireland. He meets and marries Cywair

505AD: Arthur and Cywair's sons are born around this time. They are Keidyaw, Eleuther and Greidol.

507AD: Arthur engages the Angles at the City of the Legion (Chester)

510AD: Returning north, Arthur engages the Angles at Ribchester

513AD: From his outpost at Hadrian's Wall, Arthur engages the Angles at Rochester then Edinburgh

514AD: The West Saxons come to Britain

516AD: Arthur finally defeats the Angles at Bardon

519AD: Cerdic takes Wessex

520AD: Arthur faces a rebellion from his own son Cinbelin and from his brother Morydd

534AD: Cerdic dies

539AD: Arthur fights Morydd at Camboglanna

540AD: Arthur abdicates his throne to his son Keidyaw who becomes king of Britain, ruling chiefly in the south. Eleuther rules in the north.

573AD: Gwennddolau ap Keidyaw ap Arthwys fights his cousin Peredur ap Eleuther ap Arthwys.

Evolution of the sources

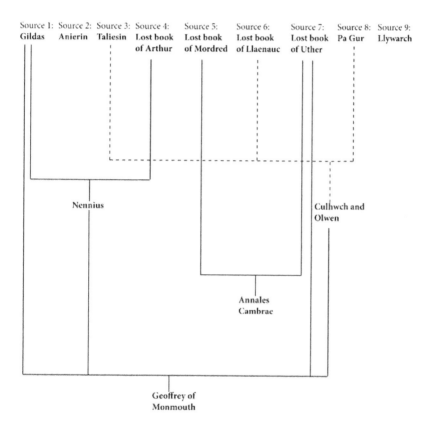

DERIVATIVE SOURCE 1

Nennius
The Historia Brittonum was edited by Nennius in around 800AD, or perhaps a little earlier. He drew on the likes of Gildas (Source 1) and used Rhun's northern chronicle (Source 4) as well as parts of the Bible and local mythology.

DERIVATIVE SOURCE 2

Annales Cambrae
The Annales does not mention Ambrosius or Vortigern, therefore it is probably not influenced by Nennius. The Annales Cambrae draws its Arthurian content from Source 5 (for the Battle of Camlann) and Source 7 (for the Battle of Arthuret and Myrddin). We should note the spelling Medraut is used.

DERIVATIVE SOURCE 3

Culhwch and Olwen
Cullhwch clearly draws upon Pa Gur (Source 8) as is seen by the inclusion of Cei, Bedwyr and the Gatekeeper. It also draws upon Source 5 for Llaeminawc and Cywair, who is called Gwenhwyfar. Culhwch is heavily influenced by the themes of Celtic mythology and Arthur's warband take on traits of legendary mythical characters. By Culhwch's time, the Britons are restricted to Wales and Cornwall, so this is where the adventures take place.

Culhwch gives us a great insight into the early King Arthur:

'Chieftain,' said Arthur, 'even though you do not say, you shall have the request that head and tongue name, as far as the wind dries, as far as the rain wets, as far as the sun rises, as far as the sea stretches, as far as the earth extends, excepting only my ship,

my mantle, my sword Caledvwlch, my spear Rhongomynyad, my shield Wynebgwrthucherm my knife Carwennan and my wife Gwwenhwyfar.'

Compare this passage in Geoffrey:

On his head he placed a golden helmet, with a crest carved in the shape of a dragon and across his shoulders a circular shield called Pridwen... He girded on his peerless sword called Caliburn, which was forged in the Isle of Avalon. A spear called Ron graced his right hand...

That Geoffrey called the sword and shield Caliburn and Ron, rather than Caledvwlch and Rhongomynyad – and called Arthur's wife Guanhumara rather than Gwenhwyfar may suggest both were working from older – but different, sources.

Culhwch sets out on his quest

DERIVATIVE SOURCE 4

Modena and Otranto

The mosaic at Otranto shows Arthur riding on the back of a goat, which may make reference to his battle at Glein (Source 4). The relief at Modena Cathedral shows him trying to rescue his wife from an enemy. It seems at this point the mythical Arthur of Cullhwch and Pa Gur has spread far and wide via Brittany.

At the center of the Modena Archivolt image is a castle defended by two towers, inside of which are two figures identified as "Mardoc" (Madog) and "Winlogee" (Guinevere or Cywair). The left tower is defended by a pickaxe-wielding man named "Burmaltus", who faces off against Artus de Bretania (King Arthur).

On the other side, the knight "Carrado" (Carados or Cerdic?) spars with "Galvagin" (Gabran or Gawain?), while "Che" (Kay) and "Galvariun" (Gwallawg or Galahad) approach with their lances at their shoulders.

"Winlogee" most likely corresponds to Arthur's wife, Guinevere. The Abduction of Guinevere is a very popular and ancient element of the Arthurian legend, first appearing in written form in Caradoc of Llancarfan's mid-12th-century Life of Gildas. What is crucial is that these carvings pre-date the European romances of Chretien and so on.

DERIVATIVE SOURCE 5

The Saints' Lives

In the saints' lives, Arthur is presented as something of a tyrant by the saints. He is accompanied by Cado (probably Cei or Cadwallon rather than Keidyaw/Cador) as well as Bedwyr and Cei. The authors of these tales care nothing for the Arthur of Badon and Camlann (Sources 1-7) and seem only interested in the grumpy old king we meet in Culhwch.

In the preface to the Legend of St. Goeznovius, the Breton writer, William, Chaplain to Bishop Eudo of Leon, gives a strong pre-Geoffrey of Monmouth potted history of Arthur. It is significant because it recalls Arthur as a conquerer of Gaul – something Geoffrey obviously did not invent.

William states that the information used in his preface came from a lost book called "Ystoria Britanica" which we know as The Lost Book Of Uther, known to William in 1019 and Geoffrey a century later.

In the course of time, the usurping king Vortigern, to buttress the defence of the kingdom of Great Britain which he unrighteously held, summoned warlike men from the land of Saxony and made them his allies in the kingdom. Since they were pagans and of devilish character, lusting by their nature to shed human blood, they drew many evils upon the Britons.

Presently their pride was checked for a while through the great Arthur, king of the Britons. They were largely cleared from the island and reduced to subjection. But when this same Arthur, after many victories which he won gloriously in Britain and in Gaul, was summoned at last from human activity, the way was open for the Saxons to go again into the island, and there was great oppression of the Britons, destruction of churches and persecution of saints. This persecution went on through the times of many kings, Saxons and Britons striving back and forth. . .

In those days, many holy men gave themselves up to martyrdom; others, in conformity to the Gospel, left the greater Britain which is now the Saxon's homeland, and sailed across to the lesser Britain (Brittany).

DERIVATIVE SOURCE 6

Lambert & William of Malmsbury

These sources and references are refreshing because they are aware of the mythical Arthur of Pa Gur/Culhwch but are more interested in preserving the memory of the Arthur of Sources 1-

7). Writing before Geoffrey, he recorded: "There is in Britain, in the land of the Picts, a palace of the warrior Arthur, built with marvellous art and variety, in which the history of all his exploits and wars is to be seen in sculpture. He fought twelve battles against the Saxons who had occupied Britain." Here it is obvious Lambert had access to Rhun or Nennius' record of Arthur's 12 battles. Lambert understands that Arthur was from the North, from his identification of Arthur as ruling the Picts.

Likewise William of Malmesbury wrote: "This is that Arthur of whom the trifling of the Britons talks such nonsense, even today; a man clearly worthy not to be dreamed of in fallacious fables, but to be proclaimed in veracious histories, as one who long sustained his tottering country and gave the shattered minds of his fellow citizens an edge for war."

DERIVATIVE SOURCE 7

Geoffrey and the Brut

Geoffrey was of a similar ilk to Lambert and William. He wanted to present Arthur as a historic king rather than some mythical deity whose warband could talk to animals and ride salmon. Geoffrey took Gildas (Source 1) for his content on the likes of Maelgwyn, he took from Nennius for his content on Vortigern and Ambrosius, and he took from the Lost Book of Uther for his content on Uther, Arthwys, Eleuther and Peredur. Geoffrey knew that Arthur was the grandson of Ceneu – he even placed Ceneu at Arthur's coronation – but at some point he decided Ceneu must have been Constantine III. Geoffrey knew Constantine III was a Roman, he knew Ambrosius was a Roman and so he assumed they were father and son.

The lineage of *Arthur I – Mar (Uther I) – Ceneu* was found in his northern chronicle.

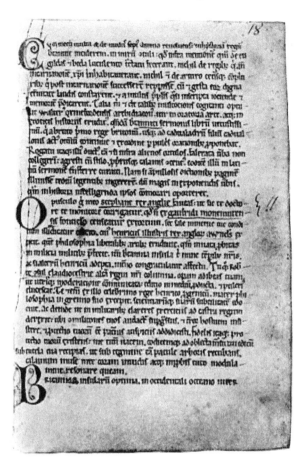

Geoffrey decided that Constantine's sons must have been brought up in Brittany, away from Vortigern.

When Geoffrey's work became the Welsh Brut chronicles, the stories were reverse-engineered into Welsh, and so Constantine became Custennin, Guanhumara went back to Gwenhwyfar and so on. Of course Geoffrey of Monmouth based his King Arthur on Arthwys ap Mar (Arthur Penuchel), but he also gave a glimpse of his direct access to northern chronicles when he mythologised Arthwys as an early ruler called Archgallo. Here Geoffrey called Mar "Morvidus" or "Morydd map Daned" and he gives him five sons, who along with Ingenius include:

Garbaniawn (based on Gwrgi)
Archgallo (based on Arthwys)
Elidurus (based on Eleuther)
Peredurus (based on Pheredur)

This shows that Geoffrey had access to northern British chronicles (which we will identify later), and when we consider that among those cited as attending Arthur's coronation were Ceneu and the son of Pabo Post Prydain, it is clear he had access to now lost information about Arthwys. Geoffrey also states that Arthur was crowned in York. And we know that at the time the king in York was Arthwys.

DERIVATIVE SOURCE 8

The Harleian and Mostyn pedigrees
In these Arthurian pedigrees Arthur I (Arthur of the Pennines) was confused was Arthur II (Arthur of Dyfed)
    There were two Kings of Britain named Arthur. King Arthur I (Arthwys ap Mar) who lived from 470-540AD and King Arthur II (Arthur ap Pedr) who lived from 565 to 645AD.
The mythical pedigree of Arthur is as follows:
Kynvor
Custennin (Flourished circa 410AD)
Uther or Iubher (Flourished circa 470AD)
Arthur (Flourished circa 500AD)
And this is actually based upon the pedigree of Arthur II whose pedigree was:
Vortipor (Flourished circa 530AD)
Congair (Flourished circa 550AD)
Retheior (Peredur, flourished circa 580AD)
Arthur II (Flourished circa 600AD)
The confusion arose because of its similarity with the pedigree of Arthur I:
Coel Hen Vortepauc (Flourished 400AD)
Ceneu (430AD)

Mar (King of Iubher) (470AD)

Arthwys (500AD)

It is easy to see how the paternal pedigree of Arthur in the Harleian and Mostyn was derived from both of these men.

DERIVATIVE SOURCE 9:

The Welsh Triads.

The Welsh Triads have become contaminated over time. Sometimes where we expect to find Arthur we do not, and where we least expect him he crops up. There are a number of the Welsh triads of interest to our study, including:

TRIAD 1

Three Tribal Thrones of the island of Britain:

Arthur as Chief Prince in Mynyw, and Dewi as Chief Bishop, and Maelgwn Gwynedd as Chief Elder;

Arthur as Chief Prince in Celliwig in Cornwall, and Bishop Bytwini as Chief Bishop, and Caradawg Strong-Arm as Chief Elder;

Arthur as Chief Prince in Pen Rhionydd in the North, and Gerthmwl Wledig as Chief Elder, and Cyndeyrn Garthwys as Chief Bishop.

Note: In Pennine Dragon, I suggested these related to Arthur holding three courts, Dyfed, Tintagel and Rheged (Penrith)

TRIAD 5

Three Pillars of Battle of the Island of Britain:

Dunawd son of Pabo Pillar of Britain,

and Gwallawg son of Lleenawg,

and Cynfelyn the Leprous.

TRIAD 6

Three Bull-Protectors of the Island of Britain:
Cynfawr Host-Protector, son of Cynwyd Cynwydion,
and Gwenddolau son of Ceidiaw,
and Urien son of Cynfarch.
Note: Cynwyd and Gwenddollau were both grandsons of Arthwys. The symbol of the VI Legion was the Bull

TRIAD 8

Three Prostrate Chieftains of the Island of Britain:
Llywarch the Old son of Elidir Llydanwyn,
and Manawydan son of Llyr Half-Speech,
and Gwgon Gwron son of Peredur son of Eliffer of the Great Retinue.
(And this is why those were called 'Prostrate Chieftains': because they would not seek a dominion, which nobody could deny to them.)
Note: Eliffer was the son of Arthwys

TRIAD 11

Three Red-Speared Bards of the Island of Britain:
Tristfardd, bard of Urien,
and Dygynnelw, bard of Owain son of Urien,
and Afan Ferddig, bard of Cadwallawn son of Cadfan.

TRIAD 12

Three Frivolous Bards of the Island of Britain:
Arthur,
and Cadwallawn son of Cadfan,
and Rahawd son of Morgant.

TRIAD 13

Three Chief Officers of the Island of Britain:
Caradawg son of Brân,
and Cawrdaf son of Caradawg,
and Owain son of Maxen Wledig.

TRIAD 14

Three Seafarers of the Island of Britain:
Geraint son of Erbin,
and Gwenwynwyn son of Naf,
and March son of Meirchiawn.

TRIAD 18

Three Battle-Horsemen of the Island of Britain:
Caradawg Strong-Arm,
and Menwaedd of Arllechwedd,
and Llyr of the Hosts.

TRIAD 20

Three Red Ravagers of the Island of Britain:
Rhun son of Beli,
and Lleu Skilful Hand,
and Morgant the Wealthy.
But there was one who was a Red Ravager greater than all three:
Arthur was his name. For a year neither grass nor plants used to
spring up where one of the three would walk; but where Arthur
went, not for seven years.

TRIAD 27

Three Enchanters of the Island of Britain:
Coll son of Collfrewy,
and Menw son of Teirgwaedd,
and Drych son of Kibddar.

TRIAD 28

Three Great Enchantments of the Island of Britain:
The Enchantment of Math son of Mathonwy (which he taught to Gwydion son of Dôn), and the Enchantment of Uthyr Pendragon (which he taught to Menw son of Teirgwaedd), and the Enchantment of Gwythelyn the Dwarf which he taught to Coll son of Collfrewy his nephew).

TRIAD 29

Three Faithful War-Bands of the Island of Britain:
The War-Band of Cadwallawn son of Cadfan, who were with him seven years in Ireland; and in all that time they did not ask him for anything, lest they should be compelled to leave him;
And the second, the War-Band of Gafran son of Aeddan, who went to sea for their lord;
And the third, the War-Band of Gwenddolau son of Ceidiaw at Arfderydd, who continued the battle for a fortnight and a month after their lord was slain.
Note: Ceidiaw was the son of Arthwys

TRIAD 30

Three Faithless War-Bands of the Islands of Britain:
The War-Band of Goronwy the Radiant of (Penllyn), who refused to receive the poisoned spear from Lleu Skilful-Hand on behalf of their lord, at the Stone of Goronwy at the head of the Cynfal;
And the War-Band of Gwrgi and Peredur, who abandoned their lord at Caer Greu, when they had an appointment to fight the next day with Eda Great-Knee; and there they were both slain;
And the War-Band of Alan Fyrgan, who turned away from him by night, and let him go with his servants to Camlan. And there he was slain.
Note: Eda was said to be the man who killed Arthur

TRIAD 54

Three Unrestrained Ravagings of the Island of Britain:
The first of them (occurred) when Medrawd came to Arthur's Court at Celliwig in Cornwall; he left neither food nor drink in the court that he did not consume. And he dragged Gwenhwyfar from her royal chair, and then he struck a blow upon her;
The second Unrestrained Ravaging (occurred) when Arthur came to Medrawd's court. He left neither food nor drink in the court;
And the third Unrestrained Ravaging (occurred) when Aeddan the Wily came to the court of Rhydderch the Generous at Alclud he left neither food nor drink nor beast alive.)

TRIAD 56

Arthur's Three Great Queens:
Gwennhwyfar daughter of Cywryd Gwent,
and Gwenhwyfar daughter of Gwythyr son of Greidiawl,
and Gwenhwyfar daughter of Gogfran the Giant.

TRIAD 57

And the Three Mistresses were these:
Indeg daughter of Garwy the Tall,
and Garwen daughter of Henin the Old,
and Gwyl daughter of Gendawd

TRIAD 59

Three Unfortunate Counsels of the Island of Britain:
To give place for their horses' fore-feet on the land to Julius Caesar and the men of Rome, in requital for Meinlas; and the second: to allow Horsa and Hengist and Rhonwen into this Island; and the third: the three-fold dividing by Arthur of his men with Medrawd at Camlan.

TRIAD 65

Three Unrestricted Guests of Arthur's Court, and Three Wanderers:
Llywarch the Old,
and Llemenig,
and Heledd

TRIAD 77

Three Wanderers of Arthur's Court:
Heledd,
and Llywarch,
and Llemenig.

TRIAD 84

Three Futile Battles of the Island of Britain:
One of them was the Battle of Goddeu: it was brought about by the cause of the bitch, together with the roebuck and the plover;
The second was the Action of Arfderydd, which was brought by the cause of the lark's nest;
And the third was the worst: that was Camlan, which was brought about because of a quarrel between Gwenhwyfar and Gwennhwyfach.
This is why those (Battles) were called Futile: because they were brought about by such a barren cause as that.

TRIAD 85

Arthur's Three Principal Courts:
Caerleon-on-Usk in Wales,
and Celliwig in Cornwall,
and Penrhyn Rhionydd (Penrith?) in the North.

TRIAD 87

Three Skilful Bards were at Arthur's Court:
Myrddin son of Morfryn,
Myrddin Emrys,
and Taliesin.

This is an appropriate Triad on which to end. Myrddin was a man of the north, grandson of Arthwys' brother. Myrddin Emrys we have identified with Arthwys' uncle Pabo, and Taliesin was a famous northern bard, serving Urien.

Source conclusions

At the start we had only the truth – that in 500AD there was only one king in Britain with 'Arth' in his name, and that was Arthwys ap Mar.

We know that this Arthwys had a brother called Llaenauc and a brother called Morydd. His wife was Cywair. He ruled the area of the country that include just North of Hadrian's Wall and down across what is now Northumbria, Yorkshire, the Pennines, Lancashire and parts of Cheshire. Within his lifetime there were 12 notable battles that took place in this region between the British and the Angles.

Northern bards and historians who either knew Arthwys, or their fathers did, recorded his exploits.

Gildas (source 1) named Badon and called a man the Bear.

Anierin (source 2) named Arthur as a valiant leader in the north against the Angles.

Taliesin (source 3) named Arthur as Gwledig at Hadrian's Wall

Rhun (source 4) named Arthur as the Dux Bellorum in 12 battles against the Angles including Badon.

These are four historically attested writers who are the primary sources for the Northern Arthur. But then we have more, and we have more because we already know who the real Arthur was.

The writer of 'the Lost Book of Mordred' (source 5) tells the story of Arthwys' civil war against his brother Morydd. We already know the Dux served at Hadrian's Wall, we know many of the 12 Battles of Rhun were around the wall, we know Taliesin stationed Arthur at the wall, and we know Moderatus was another Hadrian's Wall garrison rank. And we know that near the Wall is Camboglanna and Avallana (Camlan and Avalon) as well as Coventina's Well (the Lady of the Lake).

Next we have the writer of 'the Lost Book of Llaenauc'(source 6) who knew that Llaenauc was Arthur's closest companion and documented he and their other brother Einion on an excursion to Ireland where Arthur met Cywair and his sword Caledvwlch or Caliburn was used.

The writer of 'the Lost Book of Uther' (source 7) recorded Arthwys' father with his title Uther (derived from the word York) and his adventures against the Angles. This writer also documented Arthur's coronation in York and his being succeeded by his son Eleuther and grandson Peredur.

The original source of Pa Gur (source 8) again places Arthur in the north, fighting south of Edinburgh with his comrades Cei and Bedwyr and fighting the Angles at Celidon and Tribruit, two battles Rhun also recorded.

The northern bard Llywarch Hen (Source 9) called Arthur the imperator and tells of his commander Gereint falling in battle.

Source 10, the king lists, shows us that Arthwys was the only king of his generation that could have been King Arthur.

And from these sources, we have the original material that others worked from. Nennius got Arthur's battles from Rhun. The Annales Cambrae got battles like Camlann and Arthuret from 'the Lost Book of Mordred' and Geoffrey of Monmouth got his details from Uther to Eleuther from 'a very old book in the British tongue.'

Family Tree of the Real King Arthur

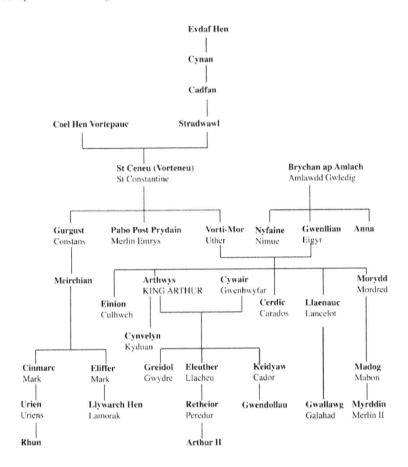

Arthur II

In both Pennine Dragon and The Lost Book of King Arthur, I make it clear that the only man who could have been Arthur was Arthwys ap Mar. For the key reasons:

He lived at precisely the right time (C470-540) to have fought at Badon in 516 and Camlann at 539.

He lived in precisely the right place – as we have identified, the earliest sources suggest that Arthur Dux Bellorum ruled from Hadrian's Wall to Chester.

He has precisely the right ancestry – descended from Coel Hen in a dynasty of Dux.

He has precisely the right family. Morydd is Mordred, Madrun is Morgan, Llaenauc is Lleminawc, Gwallawg is Galahad, Cywair is Gwenhwyfar and of course Urien and Peredur need no such explanation.

He succeeded Ambrosius Aurelianus and preceded the kings of Arthuret. In his kingdom he had a Camelot, a Camlann, a Badon, a Caerleon and more.

The strongest cases for identifying Arthur's battles puts them all around Hadrian's Wall and that's where he served. He is a better choice for a historic King Arthur than Artorius Castus (who lived 200 years too early) or Athrwys ap Meurig (who lived 200 years too late) and a man named Arthwys who ruled the kingdom around Camulod is a much more compelling subject than Owain Ddantgwyn, Cadell, Cuneglasus or Riothamus. And as a Briton he fits the bill much better than any of the Irish or Scots candidates like Artur Mac Aedan.

As I have stated on occasion, if one were to invent a time machine, go back to 516AD and ask to be taken to "King Arthur" the only man you could be taken to is Arthwys ap Mar.

But if you were to go back in that same time machine to 580AD and ask to be taken to King Arthur, the man they would take you to would be Arthur ap Pedr.

Arthur ap Pedr (Arthur ap Pets, Arthur ap Retheior, Arthur of Dyfed, Arthur of Demetia) will henceforth be known as King Arthur II.

Around the same time, Aedan Mac Gabran of Dalriada had a son called Artur, who predeceased his father, and around 60 years later, Meurig ap Tewdrig later had a son called Athrwys (Antres). There are numerous books dedicated to the theory that Artur of Dalriada was the real King Arthur, and probably just as many dedicated to the Athrwys ap Meurig hypothesis. But I find neither argument convincing. It is likely that Aedan, Pedr and Meurig named their sons 'Arthur' in tribute to the great King Arthur – and that great King Arthur was Arthwys ap Mar.

Artur of Dalriada died before his father and never became King. And as a Scot he was essentially on the opposing side to the Britons. Any of the landmarks associated with him, could better be associated with Arthwys ap Mar who lived at the right time and was a bonafide King.

Athrwys ap Meurig lived far too late to be King Arthur. Again, he predeceased his father. About the only persuasive facts about Athrwys are that he ruled near Caerleon upon Usk and he had a son called Morgan. So in Arthwys ap Mar we have a complete King Arthur, who needs no interpolations from either Artur or Athrwys. So why do I bring up the subject of Arthur II? I bring up Arthur II because like Arthur I he cannot be ignored because the details of his life are too uncanny. Secondly I would propose that the father of Arthur II Pedr ap Congair is identical with Peredur brother of Keidyaw in York and Peredur son of Cador in Dumnonia. In other words Arthur II was the great grandson of Arthwys.

Simple lineage of the two King Arthurs:
Gen 1: Coel Hen
Gen 2: Ceneu (Vortigern)
Gen 3: Mar (Vortimer)
Gen 4: Arthwys (King Arthur)
Gen 5: Eleuther
Gen 6: Peredur
Gen 7: King Arthur II

Arthur of Dyfed was not only the second king called Arthur, he was truly the second King Arthur in descent from his great grandfather Arthwys.

We do not know as much about Arthur II as we do about Arthwys but there are some records of his life that we can piece together.

The Life of Arthur II

Let us set the scene for Arthur II. The great King Arthur, Arthwys ap Mar, had died in 540AD and Britain had fallen to Saxons and British tyrants alike. By 550, most of the Britons had been pushed into what is now Wales, Devon and Cornwall. Those who ruled were tyrants like Constantine, Vortipor, Aurelius Caninus, Cuneglas and Maelgwyn. In the North, Arthur's great army was headed by his son Eleuther and his other kingdoms carved up between his sons Keidyaw and Cynvelyn.

Then, in the 560s, King Pedr of Dyfed found he was to have a son. He would call the King Arthur. The once and future king would come again and Arthur would be reborn.

Who was Arthur II?

Arthur II essentially has three possible paternal pedigrees.
The first is as follows:
Arthur son of Petur son of Congar son of Goirtiben son of Alcunn son of Tresunn son of Aed.
Spellings vary across different manuscripts and Petur is also called Retheior.

The second makes Arthur a descendant of Magnus Maximus. As instead of being the son of Aed, Triphun is the son of Clotri son of Gloitguin son of Nimet son of Dimet son of Maxim.

Each of the pedigrees agree that Arthur's father was Pedr (Pets, Petur, Retheior) who succeeded Congar (Congair, Cincar) who succeeded Goirtiben (Guartipor, Vortipor) who succeeded Alcunn (Alcol, Aircol, Agricola) who succeeded Tresun (Triphun). One genealogy inserts Erbin before Vortipor.

There is also a distinctly Romano-British feel to the names – Agricola, Vortiporus, Tribune.

The traditional theory is that they are an Irish dynasty called the Deissi who conquered Demetia, but I find it unlikely that Irish kings would all take Roman names. More likely they displaced the Irish and established their own rule.

Regardless of whether his ancestry was Welsh or Irish, Arthur succeeded Pedr who succeeded Congar who succeeded Vortipor who succeeded Agricola.

But there are two interesting anomalies with the genealogies. Firstly the Dyfed pedigree matches the Dumnonian pedigree. So we begin with Erbin, then we have Vortipor-Guartipor-Gereint , then we have Congair in Dyfed and Cador in Dumnonia, then we have Pedr in Dyfed and Peredur in Dumnonia.

Could it be therefore that Arthur II's father, grandfather, great grandfather and great great grandfather were not only kings of Dyfed they were kings of Dumnonia too? If this were the case King Arthur II would also be hereditary king of Dumnonia,

Then there is the second anomaly. Aircol in Dyfed could equate to Coel in York. Then Vortipor (Guartepir – Guarthir) could equate to Arthwys – then Congair and Cador could equate to Keidyaw. Peredur of York could be identical with Pedr of Dyfed and Peredur of Dumnonia. Therefore Arthur II would be heir to the three kingdoms. Let's consider the lineage again:

Coel (Aircol, Agricola)
Ceneu
Mar (contemporary with Erbin)
Arthwys (contemporary with Vortipor and Gereint)
Keidyaw (Congair, Cador)
Peredur, (Pedr, Retheoir)
Arthur

Were King Arthur I and King Arthur II kings of all Britain?

It is possible these two rulers were in fact national rulers. While the heartland of Arthwys was York, he may have commanded Vortipor in Dyfed and Gereint in Dumnonia – or maybe they were all the same person. It certainly seems that Arthwys' son Keidyaw of York was also known as Congair of Dyfed and Cador of Cornwall. However, at the battle of Arthuret, Keidyaw's forces were on the losing side. Commanded by his son Gwenddolau, the house of Keidyaw fell. Ironically to Keidyaw's own brother Eleuther.

Known as Eleuther of the Great Retinue (army) his forces were commanded by his son Peredur. And by seizing victory at Arthuret, Peredur became the most powerful king in Britain.

But was he so powerful he was also remembered as Pedr of Dyfed and Peredur of Dumnonia? Again it seems possible.

When Arthur II came of age, he was not only a prince of Dyfed, he was also the rightful prince of York and Dumnonia. He was heir to the throne of Britain.

We might say therefore that rather than "Arthwys of York was King Arthur and Arthur of Dyfed was King Arthur II" it is more accurate that "there were two national overkings called Arthur, one called Arthwys ap Mar and one who was his great grandson Arthur ap Pedr".

Uther Pendragon

I have reasoned that if Arthwys ap Mar was King Arthur, then surely his father Mar represents Uther Pendragon. And sure enough he has the credentials. Like Uther, Mar did his fighting in York and in Scottish pedigrees he is called Iubher (Iubher or Ebrauc means yew tree, the name of York).

But what if Arthur II was also the son of an Uther Pendragon? Arthur II's father was, in Irish pedigrees, called Retheior. If we take away Re (Ri means king) we are left with Etheuior. If we accept that Pedr was Peredur of York then his father was

Eleuther. In both Etheuior and Eleuther we can see the name Uther. Perhaps Retheior is derived from Ri Pedr ap Ri Eleuther

It is worth remembering that according to legend the lineage was Constantine-Uther-Arthur. This can be compared to Ceneu-Mar-Arthwys and Congair-Retheior-Arthur. The purpose of this chapter is not really to undermine the hypothesis that Arthwys ap Mar was King Arthur, but rather to recognise that over time, some of the exploits of King Arthur II could have been confused with his.

In the Welsh pedigrees, the one labelled X - Demetia gives a lineage of:

Erbin
Gereint
Cado
Pedur
Theudo [Tewdrig]
Peibiao
-
7 generations
Arthwael
Rees
Hewel
Eweint
Morgan

The lineage marked XI has:

Aircol [Agricola]
Erbin
Gordeber [Assumed to be Vortipor but could easily be Gereint - or both]
Kyngar
Peder
Arthur

8 generations
-
Arthwael

184

Rees
Hoel
Eweint
Morgant

What is clear is that not only was there clearly the same people on the throne of Demetia as Dumnonia.

Arthur II's historic son Noe (Noah) was born in around 600 and Noe's son Cloten was born in around 630. Cloten married Ceindrych, unifying the kingdoms of Dyfed and Brycheiniog.

"The life of King Arthur: from ancient historians and authentic documents" by Joseph Ritson records a land grant by Noe ap Arthur II which states:

NOAH (Noe), the son of Arthur, fulfilling the commandment of the apostle, saying, "Give and it shall be given to you:" and, elsewhere, as is said, "The hand extending [itself] shall not be indigent," gave, for the commerce of the celestial kingdom, in the first time, the land Pennalun, with his territory, without any assessment to [any] earthly man, but only to god and the archbishop Dubricius and Landaff, founded in honour of Saint Peter.

Was Arthur II a national King?

The confusion in the above genealogy could actually mean that Arthur II was a ruler in both Dumnonia and Dyfed, but could his reach have extended up to Scotland as well?

There are genealogies that suggest this. The first is the story of an Artur ap Bicoir fighting in Kintyre, and Artur Mac Bicoir of Kintyre could be identical with Artuir ap Pedr of Pembroke.

The first syllable in Kintyre, Pembroke and Tintagel all mean "head" as in headland. Arthurian author August Hunt, suggests Bicoir is a corruption of Petuir, as B and P can be interchanged.

Bicoir is credited with killing the Irish king Mongan mac Fiachna Lurgan in 625. The Irish Annales record:

625 Mongan, son of Fiachna of Lurga was struck with a stone by Arthur son of Bicoir the Briton, and was crushed.

So it seems that by the time of this Irish chronicle, Arthur II was synonymous with "Arthur the Briton". It has even been suggested that this was the origin of Arthur being linked to a stone (as in the sword in the stone).

About this, Bec Boirche said:

'Cold is the wind across Islay,
They shall commit a cruel deed in retribution,
They shall kill Mongan, son of Fiachna.
Where the Church of Cluan Airthir is today,
Renowned were the four there executed;
Cormac Caem, with screaming
And Illann, son of Fiachra;
And the other two, --
To whom many territories paid tribute,--
Mongan, son of Fiachna of Lurgan
and Ronan, son of Tuathal.'

One Scottish pedigree of the Clan Campbell gives *Artuir mic Iubair mic Lidir mic Brearnaird mic Muiris mic Magoth mic Coiel.*

This would appear to marry up somewhat with *Arthur son of Uther son of Eleuther son of [Arthwys] son of Mor [son of Masguid] son of Coel.*

Here it seems to the Scots genealogists 'the' King Arthur was actually Arthur II of Dyfed. A similar full pedigree states:

Dubhghaill Caimbel a quo [Muintir Chaimbeil] m. Eoghain m. Donnchaidh m. Gille Choluim m. Duibhne (o raitear Meg Dhuibhne) m. Feradaigh m. **Smerbe m. Artuir m. Iobhair m. Lidir m. Bernaird m. Muiris m. Magoth m. Coill m. Cotogain** *m. Caidimoir m. Catogain m. Bende m. Mebrec m. Grifin m. Briotain....*

or

Arthur m. Ybar m. [E]lidir m. Bernard m. Meuris m.

Magodd m. Coel m. Cadwgan m. Caid mawr m. Cadwgan m. Bende m. Mebrig m. Gryffyn m. Prydain

These lineages seem to suggest:
Coel Hen
Masguid (should be Ceneu?)
Mar
Bernard (should be Arthwys)
Eleuther
Uther II
Arthur II

So, regardless of the fact that Arthwys ap Mar was the historic King Arthur, it seems that as far as the historians in Dumnonia and Scotland were concerned, it was Arthur II they were referring to.

Campbell, in his "West Highland Tales," gives a "Genealogy Abridgment of the very ancient and noble family of Argyle, 1779."

The writer says this family began with Constantine, grandfather to King Arthur; and he informs us that Sir Moroie Mor, a son of King Arthur, of whom great and strange things are told in the Irish Traditions - was born at Dumbarton Castle, and was usually known as "The Fool of the Forest".

But these pedigrees could have come from a simple error. One could have searched pedigrees looking for a King Arthur from whom to claim descent, found Arthur ap Pedr and assumed this was Arthur Pendragon. In order for Arthur II to have contributed anything to the Arthurian legends, he must have had something to contribute.

Unfortunately we do not know the name of Arthur II's wife – so we cannot say whether she was a "Guinevere" for example. But what we can do is return to Nennius' battle list and see if any of them can be placed in the lifetime of Arthur II (roughly 565-650) rather than the lifetime of Arthur I (roughly 470-540).

Arthur I and II: The battle lists

Arthur I was the king Arthur that inspired the legend. He was the Dux at Hadrian's Wall, fighting at Glein, Badon, Camlann, Guinnion, Celidon and holding off the Angle invasion. His bravery was recorded by Aneirin, Taliesin and Rhun. Pedr, Aedan and Meurig named their sons after him. He fought civil war against his brother Morydd, ventured to Ireland with his brothers Llaenauc and Einion and was married to Cywair.

With Arthur II it is more a case of a series of what-ifs.

What if his father Pedr was actually Peredur ap Eleuther?
What if this Peredur ruled Tintagel as well as York?
What if our Arthur II set foot in Tintagel?
What if our Arthur II ruled as far north as Kintyre?
What if Arthur II was present at Arthuret?
What if Arthur II met Myrddin II?
What if Arthur II fought at the Battle of Chester, the Battle of Bindon and the Battle of the Isle of Man?

Could his father Retheior and grandfather Eleuther have added to the Uther myth?
Could his great uncle (grandfather in the pedigrees) have added t0 the Constantine myth?
Could the battle of Beandun and the battle of Bardon become intertwined in the stories of Badon?
Could the battle of Chester and the battle of City of the Legions have become intertwined?

ARTHUR I key timeline events

470AD: Born in Ebrauc to Mar and Gwenllian
489AD: Fights battle of Glein
495AD: Fights battle of Bassas
498AD: Fights battle of Celidon

501AD: Fights battle of Guinnion
513AD: Fights battle of Breguoin
516AD: Fights battle of Bardon
539AD: Fights battle of Camlann
540AD: Dies at Avalanna

Note: *Each of these battles are the ones fought around Northumbria and Hadrian's Wall. I have omitted Douglas and Tribruit (earlier identified as Wigan and Preston) and also the City of the Legions (Chester) as it is these Northumbria battles that form the strongest case for Arthwys ap Mar.*

ARTHUR II possible timeline

558AD: Born in Dyfed (or possibly York?) to Peredur
573AD: Battle of Arthuret.
Note: *If Peredur was commanding his 15-year-old son Arthur II could easily be present. If this is the case, Arthur and Merlin were at the same battle. This then could be the Battle of Celidon, since after the battle Merlin, ran into the forest.*
584AD: Battle against the Isle of Man. This battle is recorded in the Annales Cambrae immediately after the entry on the death of Peredur.
Note: *Could Arthur have fought at Douglas in the Isle of Man? Could Linnuis be Ynys? If this is the case Dubglas in the region of Linnius was Douglas in the region of Ynys Mannan*
607AD: Battle of Chester.
Note: *The date varies between about 601 and 607 in the Annales Cambrae and the Anglo Saxon Chronicle. Could this be the battle at the City of the Legions?*
614AD: Battle of Beandun (Bindon). This was a battle in which the Britons lost against the Saxons.
Note: *Could it have been confused with the victorious battle of Badon 100 years earlier?*
625AD: Arthur kills Mongan
Note: *Could this be confused with Arthwys fighting Morydd?*

Out of the 9 battle sites given by Rhun/Nennius could it be that they were fought by the two King Arthurs? It is worth noting there is no actual record of Arthur II having actually fought at any of these battles – only that they occurred in his lifetime. But it does raise the possibility that the battle lists was a combination of the two men's exploits.

ARTHUR PENUCHEL-DRACO
KING ARTHUR I

Arthur Penuchel (Arthwys ap Mar) was the original King Arthur (470-540 and fought the battle of Badon and Camlann. He was the Dux Bellorum referenced by Rhun/Nennius. Succeeding Coel, Vortigern and Ambrosius he defeated the Angles around Hadrian's Wall including Glein, Celidon, Guinnion, Bregoin, Bassas and Bardon. In his family are the real Guinevere, Lancelot, Galahad, Culhwch, Mordred and Mark. He ruled the City of the Legions and Camulod.

Parents and Kingdom:

Arthur Penuchel, otherwise known as Arthwys ap Mar was born in 470AD to the King and Queen of Iubher (Ebrauc, York) Mar and Gwenllian. Mar was the historic basis for Uther Pendragon.

Siblings:

Arthur's brothers were Morydd (Mordred), Llaenauc (Lleminauc, Lancelot), Ceretic (Cerdic, Caradoc) and Einion (Culhwch). His brothers are later recorded in the likes of the Annales Cambrae and Culhwch.

THE LADY OF THE LAKE
TELLETH ARTHVR OF THE
SWORD EXCALIBVR

Exploits:

He ruled Camulod (Camelot), Gododdin, Ebrauc, Elmet and the
Pennines and defeated the Angles in several battles in the area.
He fought at the strife of Camboglanna (Camlann) at Hadrian's
Wall against Morydd and after he died, his kingdom was lost to
Ida of Bernicia.

Family:

His Irish queen was Cywair and his sons were Greidol (Gwydre),
Cynvelyn (Amhar), Eleuther and Keidyaw (Cador).

ARTHUR PENALUN
KING ARTHUR II

Arthur ap Pedr was named after the great King Arthur and ruled from a base in Dyfed, a heartland of Arthurian legends. Flourishing almost 100 years after Arthur I, he may have contributed to the Arthurian legends based on the exploits of his great grandfather.

Parents and Kingdom:

Arthur Penalun, otherwise known as Arthur ap Pedr was born in around 560AD to the King of Dyfed Pedr. He may be identical with Arthur ap Bicoir which would mean his rule was national. His pedigree became the model for the King Arthur of Scots and

Welsh genealogies and in Ireland he was regarded as the legendary Arthur of the Britons.

Siblings:

Pedr may be identical with either Peredur of York and/or Peredur of Dumnonia. In which case Arthur may have been heir to a large kingdom. If this is the case he had brothers Gwrgi (prince of York) and Tewdwr (prince of Dumnona).

Exploits:

Although Arthur I fought the battles listed by Nennius (such as Badon), Arthur II as a young boy may have been at Arthuret in 573 in which case he may have known Myrddin (Merlin) and this could be the battle of Celidon. Arthur I could have fought at Douglas in Wigan or Arthur II at Douglas in the Isle of Man. He may have fought at the Battle of Bindun in 614. It is worth noting that Bindun was near Badbury which may be linguistically related to Badon. But this cannot be the Badon Gildas mentioned as the British did not win and it was too late. He may also have fought at the Battle of Chester (Caer Legion).

Family:

His son was Noe, (otherwise known as Nougouy and Noah). He may have also been the father of Smervie.

About the Author

Simon Keegan is the best-selling author of Pennine Dragon: The Real King Arthur of the North, and his follow-up is The Lost Book of King Arthur.

He has appeared on BBC Breakfast and BBC Look North with his Arthurian discoveries.

A journalist for around 20 years, he has written for several national newspapers and magazines.

He read medieval history at St John Rigby College.

A keen genealogist, he is descended from Arthwys ap Mar on his mother's side (see chart in Pennine Dragon) and from Niall of the Nine Hostages on his father's side (confirmed by Y Chromosome DNA testing). His family the Clann MacAodhagain (Clan Mac Keegan) were the hereditary chief bards, historians and lawmakers of Ireland (Brehon and Ollamh) documented in the Annales of the Four Masters. The clan's castle, Redwood Castle, was said to be the oldest clan castle in Ireland still in possession of its original clan.

Index